The Shadow Government:

9-11 and State Terror

D0862140

SEND $1.00 FOR CATALOG
Bohica Concepts
P.O. Box 546, Dept. LAB
Randle, Wash. 98377

Len Bracken

(with Andrew Smith)

The Shadow Government: 9-11 and State Terror

© 2002 by Len Bracken
Introduction © 2002 by Kenn Thomas

ISBN 1-931882-05-3

First Printing September 2002

All Rights Reserved

Photographs by Len Bracken

Printed in the United States of America

Published by
Adventures Unlimited Press
One Adventure Place
Kempton, Illinois 60946 USA

www.adventuresunlimitedpress.com
www.adventuresunlimited.nl
www.wexclub.com

10 9 8 7 6 5 4 3 2

Dedicated to Christine and Carla

THE
SHADOW
GOVERNMENT

CONTENTS

THE
SHADOW
GOVERNMENT

Acknowledgements

This book depends on reporting by many writers we would not have discovered without Rob Sterling's invaluable Konformist Newswire—sources such as Michael Ruppert of From the Wilderness; Tom Flocco, UnansweredQuestions.org; Jared Israel, Emperor's New Clothes; Greg Palast, BBC; and Michel Chossudovsky. The book began as a conspectus on *Ben Laden La Vérité Interdite* by Jean-Charles Brisard and Guillaume Dasquié; we then investigated their sources and arrived at a few different conclusions. The notes indicate our indebtedness to authors James Bamford, Alan Freidman, David Hoffman, Rhodri Jeffreys-Jones, Jim Keith, Gianfranco Sanguinetti, Christopher Simpson, Anthony Sutton, and Philip Willan. We relied on Ahmed Rashid's *Taliban* for background. The book also benefited from researchers such as John Judge from COPA; Robert Parry, Consortium; Jim Fleming, Autonomedia; Joan d'Arc, *Paranoia*; Gordon Thomas, Globe-Intel; Daniel Brandt, NameBase; Peter Kornbluh, National Security Archives; Ian Willams Goddard in *Prevailing Winds*; and Stephanie Reich in *Covert Action Quarterly*, although this is not to suggest that anyone mentioned above necessarily endorses our work. Our anthrax chapter drew from the writers and editors of the *Hartford Courant*, especially Jack Dolan and Dave Altimari, who courageously researched and published information about the activities of government scientists at Fort Detrick, Maryland. We recognize Richard J. Ochs for his decades of uncovering the corrupt and murderous practices of the US Government and for his research into the suspicious timing of the 2001 anthrax attacks on the Freedom From Terror website. Barbara Hatch Rosenberg, Ph.D., chair of the Federation of American Scientists Working Group on Biological Weapons, professor at the State University of New York, Purchase, has been at the forefront of scientists speaking out from inside the establishment. Judith Miller, Stephen Engelberg, and William Broad of the *New York Times* served us and the public well with their investigation into the US government's biological warfare program. We would also like to express our gratitude to Amy Goodman and Ambrose I. Lane Sr. for their WPFW broadcasts on numerous subjects. Ben Bacon, Michael Zarowny, Jenny Mittelstaedt, and Steve Taylor contributed editorial expertise. Apologies and thanks to anyone we may have forgotten. The book would not exist without the good graces of Kenn Thomas, *Steamshovel Press*, and the courage of Adventures Unlimited publisher David Childress.

Foreword

Shallow Government—Nobody in Charge
By Kenn Thomas

Nobody won the election of 2001 and everybody knows this. Al Gore didn't win or he'd be president. George Bush, whose reported latest gaffe (that the French have no word for *entrepreneur*) adds to his legend as America's most stupid pretender to the presidency,[1] was appointed to that post by the Supreme Court in a bad decision cast along very narrow ideological lines.[2]

History already has filed away the short version of that election: Gore got the popular vote and the shadows—Bush family and cronies—shanghaied the electoral vote in Florida. Never before had conspiracy politics been pushed so into the face of American citizens. Extra-electoral power politicking with a trail going back to the Bush build up and break down of Saddam Hussein, back to Iran-contra, back further to the Reagan assassination attempt, to the October Surprise, on back to the Kennedy assassination, back further even to the Nazis. Same players. Same shadow government.[3] Nobody was the real winner.

The concept of the "shadow government," in fact, played a public relations role in the activities of the new ersatz administration just after 9-11. It publicly acknowledged the underground bunkers that members of an alternate administration would occupy in case the "real" one was wiped out by some terrorist attack. The only irony acknowledged by the compliant press was that the computers in these secret bunkers needed upgrading. The bigger irony remained, that the notion of hidden underground bunkers housing the true manipulators of the world, a long-held concept by students of conspiracy and parapolitics, had long been laughed at as the product of crazy, paranoid minds.

The September 11 attacks granted a new legitimacy to that idea, to the idea of sleeper agents, mind-controlled assassins, the terror mirror of interlocking state spy bureaucracies and global killer terrorist networks, to the whole gamut of conspiracy theory ideas that before had seemed so far-fetched. Many had previously argued that conspiracy theory (more properly called, for the sake of clarity, the study of parapolitics) sought falsely to impose order on a chaotic universe. It seemed clear to more people after 9-11 that the chaos was coming from somewhere and that its discernible roots stretched outside the instantly declared enemies of the state.[4] It could not be the fault of the elected officials because, after all, Nobody had won the previous election.

Few people understand this better than the Baltimore-Washington Psychogeographic Association (BWPA), whose diligent research pieced together this remarkable amassing of theories and facts on the 9-11 disaster. The book's authors, Len Bracken and Andrew Smith, along with other BWPA members launched the Campaign for Nobody in Baltimore's Inner Harbor as early as 1999. With little more than some leafleting of Baltimore, Washington, and Philadelphia, the group led the charge that culminated in their candidate taking over America in the fall of 2001, when Nobody won. Late night talk show talker Conan O'Brien even mentioned the group in his monologue as "anarchists who look like everyone else."

Bracken is known in the marginal circles as a biographer, essayist, novelist, and translator. Smith was a pioneer in the American *samizdat* style zine revolution with his publications *Underground Beat* and *Reality Sandwich*. His writing has appeared in numerous independent and small-press publications, including, most recently, *Fifth Estate*, North America's longest-running continually published anarchist periodical. The collaborators are reticent to discuss division of labor except to say that Smith wrote the anthrax chapter and Bracken the state-terror thesis.

Of all the conspiracy theories put forth since 9-11, the state terror thesis is the simplest, most elegant and most easily followed. The basic notion is that whether or not it actually participates in any given mass crime event, like 9-11 or the Oklahoma City bombing, the state uses these occasions as a means to consolidate and expand its power. Everywhere today, the upshot of the WTC and Pentagon plane crashes has been an extraordinary erosion of cherished American civil rights through the creation of ever more powerful police bureaucracies, such as the new Homeland Security Department, and the application of human and economic resources for an ill-defined and never-ending war. It is easy enough to see. People are put on ever more imaginary degrees of alert and the prospect of military takeover of civilian police functions is openly considered. Yet few expect the bureaucratic bloat to have much impact on the next real terror attack.

But does it end there? Is it simply a matter of the power-mad elite taking advantage of the misguided actions of dispossessed, insane terrorists? As a compendium of the facts about 9-11 alone, *Shadow Government* follows these questions to their inevitable conclusion: that the state participates in the events it exploits. Given the history of how useful acts of terror became in enhancing state power, it only makes sense that in time the state would orchestrate such acts. For readers who might find it a difficult proposition to accept, consider lessons in the spectacle of power abuse paraded repeatedly on television: the Rodney King and Donovan Jackson videos—yes, They can do that to one or two ordinary citizens; the Zapruder film—yes, They can do THAT to someone people thought they elected; 9-11—can They do that to such a large group of ordinary citizens? *Shadow Government* presents the historical backdrop and the current body of research that makes this proposition credible. It is important reading in a world adrift, as Nobody serves out the term.

Notes:

1. Prior to 9-11 Mark Crispin Miller's *The Bush Dyslexicon* collected misstatements, crudities and ignorant arrogance made by Bush in various public and media forums. To his credit, Miller produced a new edition after 9-11, when the implications of having such an inadequate chief executive seemed far less humorous.

2. I heard news of the decision while standing on the corner of Bush and Mason streets in San Francisco, pondering the synchronicity. Two weeks later, while visiting author Bracken in DC, I had my first opportunity to attend a Supreme Court proceeding, when respect for the institution was perhaps at its lowest point in history.

3. A bibliography of books that outline some of the secret history involving the current president and his family should perhaps begin with Fortunate Son by J. H. Hatfield. Hatfield was a celebrity biographer found dead shortly after Bush family efforts to stop publication of his book, which included material about the president's drug and alcohol habits, failed. Peter

Brewton's *The Mafia, CIA and George Bush* (Shapolsky, 1992) helped sound the clarion call on the senior Bush. It included information regarding Jim Bath, a good friend and real estate business partner to the current president, Bush Jr. Bath was a trustee for the two wealthiest families in Saudi Arabia, one of them a money conduit for Adnan Khasshoggi during his partnership with Manucher Gorbanifar. Khasshoggi and Gorbanifar managed the Iran-contra arms-for-hostages deal, and came under the research scrutiny of Danny Casolaro. As Dodi Fayed's uncle, Khasshoggi was also noted for his connection to the assassination of Princess Diana. (See: *The Octopus* by Kenn Thomas and Jim Keith, Feral House, 2003.)

4. Definitive proof of Osama Bin Laden's involvement with the 9-11 disasters has never been offered. Neither have adequate reasons why the resources of the world police agencies failed to capture such a feeble man, afflicted with osteoporosis and kidney problems requiring dialysis. The identities of the plane hijackers remain disputed and officially most of them primarily came from Saudi Arabia, a US ally. After the plane crashes stopped all other air traffic in the country, a single plane made stops throughout the country to pick up members of Bin Laden's family and escorted them out of the country.

"Any of the contrived situations described above are inherently, extremely risky in our democratic system in which security can be maintained, after the fact, with very great difficulty. If the decision should be made to set up a contrived situation it should be one in which participation by US personnel is limited only to the most highly trusted covert personnel. This suggests the infeasibility of the use of military units for any aspect of the contrived situation." US Joint Chiefs of Staff, plans for Operation Northwoods [1]

---

[1] Cited in James Bamford, *Body of Secrets* (New York, 2002), 89.

Preface

The Baltimore-Washington Psychogeography Association brought you the Campaign for Nobody in 2000 when nobody won more convincingly than ever. Now we test, as is appropriate for the essay form, the hypothesis that the United States government played a malevolent role in the nearly flawless September 11, 2001 operation and subsequent anthrax attacks. Four teams of skyjackers crashed two planes into the World Trade Center, one into the Pentagon, and lost a fourth plane in Pennsylvania under disputed circumstances. Anthrax-laced letters sent to people in several locales, primarily in the Washington metropolitan area, terrorized the nation. Our intention is to either confirm or deny the *X-Files* suspicions of people on the street.

It is not "second guessing," as President Bush says, nor is it "beyond the pale," as Vice President Cheney claims, for us to ask obvious questions about what these statesmen and others knew and when they knew it. The fact, widely reported in the mainstream press, that the White House acknowledged its lie about a phone call warning of a threat against Air Force One on the day of the attack invites questions about all its assertions. If you lie once, it is only reasonable for us to assume you will do so again. We also extend this patriotic skepticism to Defense Secretary Rumsfeld, CIA Director Tenet, FBI Director Mueller, and Joint Chiefs Chairman Meyers.

If those in high places smart from the facts presented here or at our theoretical assertions, they can easily refute them to relieve the sting. Maybe we're wrong on more than a few minor errors of fact, inevitable in a time of widespread disinformation, and guilty of gross misinterpretation. Perhaps these statesmen and their epigones can prove that we are often mistaken, that our implausible argument lacks continuity, or perhaps we will receive clarification from these statesmen on the falsity of our misguided categories. If, however, they are unable to deny their malfeasance in the honest terms we use here, then they should resign or be driven from office.

To those who would dismiss our argument out of hand on the grounds that no statesman could be so cruel, we remind them that the world has experienced the likes of Nero, who set fire to Rome in 64 AD Suetonius, who uses the word *terror* in reference to the event, attributes the act to Nero's decadent tastes, which he and other historians extend to the emperor enjoying the macabre spectacle of ten of the city's fourteen districts being consumed in a weeklong blaze.[1] Historians like to tell the story of Nero singing "Fall of Illium" from the Tower of Maecenas, but they often neglect to mention his intention to terrorize Christians

---

[1] Suetonius, *The Twelve Caesars* (New York, 1957), 230–31.

who claimed all were equal before God and thus challenged the Roman slave system.

As was the case wherever statesmen met or attempted to meet around the turn of the millennium, in July 2001, protesters, this time a quarter-million, marched in Genoa against globalization and rising inequality. This G8 summit revealed what statesmen considered to be their threats: 1) a skyjacked plane used as a suicide bomb against Air Force One or any building known to contain President Bush, and 2) the moral and biological force of the masses in the street, particularly the anarchist black bloc. The first threat and the response of closing airspace around the city to commercial traffic demonstrate that security forces knew this tactic was possible. The second threat and the response—bringing in Nazi skinhead provocateurs from Germany and England posing as black bloc anarchists while destroying mom and pop shops—reveals what dishonest and terrorist lengths statesmen will go to oppose the anti-globalization movement.

Evidence of these provocations—captured on video by authentic protesters, who were routinely attacked by the thugs, and by independent filmmakers—led to opposition senators walking out on the response by the minister of interior. He survived a no-confidence vote, but quickly removed the police superintendent of Genoa, the deputy chief of police in charge of the G8 meeting, and the national head of the antiterrorism department. These measures were designed to mask the direct

19

relationship, reported by *Der Spiegel* and elsewhere, of national politicians with the neofascist Northern Alliance ensconced at *carabinieri* headquarters in Genoa during the protest.

Yale professor David Graeber documented the terror in a cover story for *In These Times*; other reports also reveal that a particularly bloody surprise attack on protest headquarters was carried out by a unit trained by Los Angeles police sheriffs on the use of aluminum batons. An anonymous officer dared to speak about this attack by his fellow policemen to the mainstream daily, *La Republica*: "They urinated on one person. They beat people up if they didn't sing Facetta Nera. One girl was vomiting blood, but the chief of the squad just looked on. They threatened to rape girls with their batons." The Independent Media Center in Genoa documented the carnage, such as the shooting to death and running over of a protester by the *carabinieri*, and the IMC was raided—at midnight with tear gas and batons. Eyewitnesses say that as the black bloc impostors burned cars and smashed shop windows like soccer hooligans, they were escorted by the *carabinieri*, who even waited outside while a bank was being burned. *La Republica* interviewed a purported anarchist, Liam 'Doggy' Stevens from Birmingham, England: "I'm a Nazi, not an anarchist. I don't care about the G8 or anti-globalization bullshit. The Italian brothers invited me. They told me we wouldn't have troubles with the police—they would allow us to do all we wanted."[1]

For those who argue our first example is too long ago and the second still too far away, we have a few reminders. The United States government massacred the First Nations and sanctioned slavery—racist atrocities that dwarf horrors at the World Trade Center and Pentagon in September 2001. We will focus on a more recent and poignant example to remind those with confidence in the virtues of state authority, an example concerning state involvement in the events surrounding the attack on the World Trade Center in 1993.

The CIA consciously assisted the entry of the blind cleric Sheikh Omar Abdel Rahman into the United States, where he established a mosque in Jersey City, because of his sway with the mujahadeen. Rahman's conspiracy trial revealed that the US Army Special Forces Sergeant Ali A. Mohammed trained Mahmud Abouhalima[2] in Jersey City—Abouhalima was later convicted for his role in the World Trade Center bombing.[3] The man who purportedly planted the bombs, Mohammed Salameh, was likewise one of the blind sheikh's followers, although his post-bombing attempts to obtain his security deposit for the

---

[1] See Suggested Reading.
[2] Perhaps more correctly, Mahmood Abu Halima.
[3] Peter Waldman and Frances A. McMorris, "The Other Trial: As Sheik Omar Case Nears End, Neither Side Looks Like a Winner," *Wall Street Journal*, September 22, 1995.

truck rented in his name, which he reported stolen, indicate that he was set up.

Police arrested Salameh as he left the Jersey City Ryder rental center and the FBI alleged that his rental papers were covered with traces of chemical nitrates. We have yet to hear a viable reason why, if he were guilty of the World Trade Center bombing, Salameh returned to the Ryder rental center. Moreover, the *Washington Post* reported and court proceedings confirmed that the FBI's crime laboratory fabricated evidence in the case.[1] Special Agent Frederic Whitehurst testified that he was pressured to support the preliminary theory that a urea nitrate bomb was used in the explosion, to support the prosecution case, even though he disagreed with this assertion.

The FBI located the bomb-making factory in the Jersey City apartment of a person named Josie Hadas, who somehow completely escaped prosecution.[2] Was the real bomber protected and a patsy prosecuted? Rather than directly attacking terrorists, what in strategic terms is a direct defensive attack, did government or cut out operations indirectly attack the public under a false flag?

We have still more convincing suggestions that the FBI collaborated in the conspiracy to blow up the World Trade Center in 1993. Emad Eli Salem, an Egyptian military man who was a double agent for Egypt and the United States, served as

---

[1] *Washington Post*, September 14, 1995.
[2] *International Herald Tribune*, June 8, 1993.

Sheikh Omar's security guard while performing the FBI roles of informant and agent provocateur. He secretly recorded conversations with his FBI handlers, which were in part reprinted in the *Wall Street Journal* and *New York Times*.[1]

What emerges from these tapes is that the FBI instructed Salem to recommend targets and show the terrorists how to build a truck bomb. Salem resented being taken off the case and told his FBI handlers that the bombing could have been avoided—they, bureau agents John Anticev and Nancy Floyd, agreed. The former dissuaded Salem from reporting to Washington about this intelligence lapse that killed six and injured hundreds by a cyanide truck bomb. What happened, as we now know, was that after Salem was pulled off the case, Iraqi intelligence agent Ramzi Yousef filled the void. This must have troubled the FBI because they immediately questioned, but did not arrest, many of Sheikh Omar's cohorts.

Instead the FBI inexplicably lowered the level of their surveillance with the advent of Yousef's participation, when they knew terrorist plans were known to be underway. *Sixty Minutes*, on May 31, 2002, reports that a member of the terrorist team, Abdul Rahman Yassin, was picked up after the attack. Reportedly because he was so cooperative, the FBI drove him home and released him. Yassin promptly escaped. As if it needed it, the FBI was granted still wider range to carry out investigations and

---

[1] Reprinted in David Hoffman, *Oklahoma City Bombing and the Politics of Terror* (Venice, 1998).

prevent attacks after this first World Trade Center bombing, and it did so often dishing out abuse on thin evidence. But somehow, for some reason, the FBI let terrorists go, protected them. What did Ramzi Yousef know, or was he boasting, when the helicopter transporting him to trial in Manhattan swooped over the World Trade Center and the FBI man lowered his shroud? To the taunt that he failed to destroy the building, Yousef responded, "Not yet."

In light of the facts surrounding the 1993 bombing of the World Trade Center, and the evidence associated with the 2001 suicide skyjackings, we have to ask ourselves if history has repeated itself. Events unfold in a particular way, so we are amazed when this particularity repeats itself, when other events have aspects identical to those that preceded them. It strikes us as the height of absurdity to accept this repetition and its consequences. That would be as if we were living in the Middle Ages when history and the state were believed to be functions of divine will.

Renaissance thinkers held that social and state forms are the work of humans, works of art, according to Swiss historian Jacob Burckhardt.[1] If we can find something of the past lurking in the present, let it be the ability to give more virtuous shape to history as it unfolds than contemporary statesmen who would have history resemble Voice of America television propaganda that

---

[1] Jacob Burckhardt, *Civilization of the Renaissance in Italy* (London, 1990).

24

spectators view but never live. Toward the end of his first chapter, The State as a Work of Art, Burckhardt reminds us that Machiavelli called for a judicial procedure against hated citizens to replace the informal court of scandal. Some way, in any event, must be devised to deal with the traitors who perpetrate these wounds on fellow citizens.

Many readers who thought they knew the truth about the 1993 World Trade Center bombing are astonished by the facts presented above and would like to dismiss the notion that the first bombing resembles the second in the complicity of the state. They refuse to believe that the US government used its citizens to test its germ warfare program on civilian populations in Minneapolis, St. Louis, New York, and San Francisco, and therefore should be questioned about its responsibility for the anthrax attacks.[1] A lawsuit by postal workers notes that members of the White House staff began taking Cipro prior to the anthrax attacks, as if they knew these attacks were coming, and failed to alert the public. We extend our apologies to those disturbed by this, but nothing can be any different than it was. We're compelled to attach to this prefatory note a message for those whose doubts and beliefs may be misplaced, which should be read with the book's epigraph from the Joint Chiefs in mind. A realistic message from our favorite Renaissance writer, Machiavelli, in the form of a dialogue, on the *Art of War*:

---

[1] Leonard Cole, *Clouds of Secrecy* (Totowa, 1988).

25

On this topic I maintain that since this is a profession by means of which men cannot live honestly at all times, it cannot be carried on as a profession except in a republic or in a kingdom. Neither of these governments, when it is well organized, has ever allowed any of its citizens or subjects to practice it as a profession. Nor has any good man ever taken it up as his own particular profession. For a man will never be judged good who, in his work—if he wants to make a steady profit from it—must be rapacious, fraudulent, violent, and exhibit many qualities that, of necessity, do not make him good. Nor can men who practice war as a profession—great men as well as insignificant men—act in any other way, since their profession does not prosper in peacetime. Such men must either hope for no peace or must profit from times of war in such a manner that they can live off the profit in times of peace. Neither of these thoughts is found in a good man, for the desire to be able to support oneself at all times leads to theft, acts of violence, and the murderous deeds that such soldiers perpetrate on their friends and foes alike. … Have you not read that the Carthaginian soldiers, at the end of the first war with the Romans—under Matho and Spedius (two leaders chosen by them from the mob)—waged a more dangerous war against the Carthaginians than they had just finished waging against the Romans?[1]

Times have changed and we know that some contemporary professional military personnel, unlike the mercenaries denounced by Machiavelli, serve with honor and distinction. The monster that resides in all of us has been cultivated in these soldiers, yet they seemingly control it through community

---

[1] Niccolò Machiavelli, *Art of War* (New York, 1995), 13–14.

constraints or vent in acceptable ways, such as in sports. The serial murders of special operations' wives in Fort Bragg, North Carolina in summer of 2002 gives us a portrait of the monster from the carnage left behind. As much as we would like to kill the entire military service enterprise, on moral grounds, we acknowledge it as a necessity in this state-based world order when humans behave like monsters. We deeply resent, however, the military and paramilitary FBI and CIA when they deceive us like dangerously disloyal mercenaries devoid of allegiance to fellow citizens.

A timely new book confirms in a public and clear way what has been known in research and opposition circles for years. The prevalent tradition in American intelligence history is for fast-talking confidence men to always push for the expansion of their covert operations, according to a professor of American history from Edinburgh. In *Cloak and Dollar*, Rhodri Jeffreys-Jones makes the following observation:

Another bizarre and oft-repeated practice has been the reward of failure. A disaster happens: the government sets up a preemptive inquiry to deliberate until the fuss dies down; the confidence men now say the disaster happened because they had too little money to spend on intelligence; the president and Congress authorize more intelligence funds. Thus, for example, Pearl Harbor spawned the OSS and CIA, and the National Security

Agency's shortcomings in the 1990s inspired not punitive cuts but larger appropriations.[1]

Jeffreys-Jones presents compelling information regarding intelligence reform in the wake of the September 2001 attacks. He even goes so far as to say "the situation was custom-made for the intelligence confidence man and his political allies." The professor, however, pulls his punches and mildly exhorts the US intelligence community "to become more a part of the wider world." We prefer Renaissance vehemence because it is the literary tradition that matches our moral indignation, and because Machiavelli's mercenary theme matches the reality of 9-11: he singles out Hiero of Syracuse, who, when he realized he could neither keep nor disband disloyal troops, had them cut to pieces.

We can debate the degree of foreknowledge on the part of US citizens inside and outside of government, but there is no denying that Israel was on top of the skyjacking operation—the leaks authorized by Prime Minister Ariel Sharon attest that he warned Bush. Thomas Gordon writes about this in a well-sourced article entitled "Bush: The Ignored Warning That Will Come to Haunt Him," (*Globe-Intel* May, 24, 2002), which reports on articles by himself and Yvonne Ridley in Washington for *Sunday Express* (London). According to Thomas, his sources and documents shown to Ridley indicate that Mossad did not withhold information. Other disclosures, such as the arrest of

---

[1] Rhodri Jeffreys-Jones, *Cloak and Dollar* (New Haven, 2002), 9.

tens if not hundreds of Israeli agents posing as art students across the country in a vast spy dragnet just prior to 9-11, point to close coverage by Mossad of the entire affair.[1] Either Israeli intelligence behaved like disloyal mercenaries to their most generous ally, the United States, and withheld information, which it denies. Or else the executive branch of the US government has a staunch ally and knew much more than it admits.

We will come back to this aspect of the case—the Mossad surveillance and possible infiltration of the skyjackers operation, along with the warnings to the CIA from British MI6 and German BND. For now we merely note that both the United States and Israel read the events of 9-11 as a green light on terrorism: one to pursue terrorists in Afghanistan and build an oil pipeline, the other to pursue terrorists in Palestinian refugee camps to annex more of the West Bank for greater Israel. We think it is only fair to ask if they reached behind their backs and flipped the switch.

Sharon's first major strike prior to the spring 2002 offensive may have been against former Lebanese Christian warlord Elie Hobeika (alternately Elie Hobeiqa), reported executor of the 1982 massacres at Sabra and Shatila Palestinian refugee camps. An Israeli commission placed indirect responsibility on Sharon because he allowed Christian militiamen

---

[1] See Suggested Reading.

to enter the camps in what looks to us like the stratagem of killing with a borrowed knife. Sharon, who resigned as defense minister because of the scandal, faces possible war crimes charges in Belgium for the massacres. Hobeika, who had twice been elected to Lebanon's parliament, agreed to testify. His car was blown up as it passed a remote-controlled car bomb parked curbside in what the head of Lebanon's military court said was another Israeli cross-border assassination. [1]

---

[1] Howard Schneider, "Blast Kills Ex-Commander Tied to Lebanon Massacre," *Washington Post,* January 25, 2002.

I.

State-Terror Thesis

"The deceiver by stratagem leaves it to the person whom he is deceiving to commit the errors of understanding that at last, flowing into *one* result, suddenly change the nature of things in his eyes. We may therefore say, as wit is sleight of hand with ideas and conceptions, so stratagem is sleight of hand with actions."

Carl von Clausewitz, *On War*

1.

We would rather enjoy and praise this world than oppose it. The dangerous schemes our statesmen use to obtain what they by no means deserve prevent us, for the moment, from relaxing or writing about men and women who set good examples. We understand how terrorism has worked and obtain no satisfaction from knowing about stratagems others don't know about or pretend not to know about. Our social conscience has been stirred by the sinister facts that have emerged surrounding the events of September 11, 2001 and we see the need to establish the record, as it stands, near the one-year mark.

Unlike the children of all ages who believe what they are told and do as they're told because they believe authorities know best and do what is best, we don't overestimate what is known; we draw logical conclusions from existing evidence about the way terrorists and their financiers were repeatedly protected and the way statesmen deceived us. Wars often involve ruses and if we accept the state's narrative, 9-11 was a relatively simple stratagem, what ancient Asian theorists of war called hiding a knife, in this case box cutters, behind a smile. The heretical narrative on 9-11 inquires whether we have been deceived more or less by statesmen who turned a blind eye to the attacks in a wolfish stratagem designed to lead the public astray, as if it were a passing herd of sheep. When we see how statesmen continue to frighten the public with straw men, as a diversion from an investigation into the Black Tuesday attacks, we have to ask if these statesmen killed with borrowed knives. In other words, we wonder whether the massacres in New York and Virginia were engendered or facilitated by statesmen in order to silence opposition, consolidate power, and rally the population behind a war favorable to military and oil industries.

Merely by broaching the subject of the state indirectly attacking, or allowing an attack, on citizens it should defend, we stand accused of being conspiracy theorists, a label we neither accept nor reject because we are independent historians and

34

strategic theorists who do not share the widespread academic prejudice against conspiracies. "So strong is this prejudice among academics," historian Jeffrey Bale writes, "that even when clear evidence of a plot is inadvertently discovered in the course of their own research, they frequently feel compelled, either out of a sense of embarrassment or a desire to defuse anticipated criticism, to preface their account of it by ostentatiously disclaiming a belief in conspiracies."[1]

We identified the first conspiracy in history, by the way, by looking only as far as the first chapter of *Histories* by Herodotus, father of the field. All contemporary covert operations would be considered to be conspiracies by Machiavelli. The fact that Zacorias Moussaoui,[2] the so-called twentieth hijacker, is on trial for conspiracy demonstrates that at least the judiciary recognizes the event for what it was, a conspiracy, although it may limit the scope to protect the state. We dismiss the academic prejudice and instead trust Machiavelli's discourse on conspiracies that asserts "many more princes have lost their lives and their states in this way than by open war."[3] The strategic theorist from Percussina holds that prudence is the only requirement for certain success in conspiracies formed by the strong and that conspiracies against one's country are less dangerous than most.

---

[1] Cited in Robin Ramsay, *Conspiracy Theories* (Harpenden, 2002), 12.
[2] Alternately, Zakaria Mousaouie.
[3] Niccolò Machiavelli, *Discourses* (New York, 1983), 398.

2.

Our conspiracy-minded suspicions, based on Machiavelli's formulations in the sixth of his *Discourses,* and those of his descendents, bolstered by historical evidence, lead us to the state-terror thesis. The contradictory statements by US statesmen and women about what was known prior to the attacks, and the admission by White House spokesman Ari Fleisher in May 2002 that new threat warnings were used to allay criticism about 9-11 warnings, prove, at the very least, that men and women of state produced fear in the public for cynical ends. We remember how often the lie was repeated that the government had no idea terrorists would use skyjacked planes as missiles when the notion was mentioned in reports, memos, terrorist plans, video games, and a Tom Clancy novel.[1]

The people in positions of authority would have us believe that al-Qaeda was invincible and the FBI inept. They would have us forget that threats and plans were made to invade Afghanistan prior to the attack; that an unprecedented US-British naval exercise, operation Swift Sword, was underway in the Arabian Sea in September 2001; that simultaneously in Egypt, the NATO operation Bright Star, with more than 23,000 troops, brought the

---

[1]   Tom Clancy, *Debt of Honor* (New York, 1994).

total of those involved in the two operations to more than sixty
thousand troops. We have not forgotten and we are not afraid of
accusing statesmen of producing fear, like slaveholders, except
insofar as this dissent may earn us false accusations of supporting
terrorism.

We want to make it clear that we vehemently oppose
terrorism on principle while we nonetheless recognize its tactical
successes and failures without moral judgment. We critically
examine the recurring circumstances and logic behind events
such as Pearl Harbor and 9-11 for ostensibly turning a blind eye
to surprise attacks. The fear-induced servitude of a mystified
public that predictably spread across the land after the first and
second bombings of the World Trade Center, as well as the
Oklahoma City bombing, make us question the state's suspicious
withdrawal of informants and surveillance prior to the attacks and
the state's proven and possible use of provocateurs and
infiltrators.

The consequences of these events, in our opinion, betray
reason. Self-inflicted wounds, or what amount to them, become
the rationale for expanded roles and funding for agencies that
routinely dissimulate and deploy ruses on civilians, namely the
CIA, FBI, and military intelligence. Excess espionage begets still
more privacy-invading espionage. Machiavelli counsels from the
sixteenth century that our martial and political lives are blurred
beyond distinction. With him, we judge people for how they act
in worst-case scenarios and say to our statesmen, like the blind

37

prophet to Oedipus, you are the murderer you hunt with your agent provocateurs and other stratagems.

3.

We have had the good fortune to come across the undeservedly obscure works of a Machiavellian from another generation and the events that made his writing necessary.[1] One could not exist without the other, and although we have already written about Gianfranco Sanguinetti and the strategy of tension in Italy,[2] we reprise him and his time because they clearly reveal how and why states use false-flag operations.

A most remarkable and rare book on the subject is *Puppetmasters: The Political Use of Terrorism in Italy* by Philip Willan, a writer we admire for his abilities and his courage. This British journalist, based in Rome, describes Sanguinetti as a maverick but nonetheless presents his offensive-defensive terror dichotomy in support of the assertion that terrorism was used by the state to maintain social order by constant pressure. Sanguinetti divides terrorism into the offensive form, used by groups such as the IRA and PLO, and the defensive form, used by the state to

---

[1] Gianfranco Sanguinetti, *On Terrorism and the State* (London, 1982), *The Real Report on the Last Chance to Save Capitalism in Italy*, (Fort Bragg, 1997).
[2] Len Bracken, *Guy Debord—Revolutionary* (Venice, 1997); idem, *Arch Conspirator*, (Kempton, 1999).

directly attack its citizens, or to do so indirectly under the guise of either left-wing or right-wing extremist groups, or by allowing an attack to happen or other variants. Offensive terror is an ineffective tactic because it tends to turn off the population the group should instead win over and actually stiffens the resolve of those confronted with it. For this reason indirect defensive attacks tend to work out well for the established power.

Offensive terrorist organizations are so weak and organized in such a way that the state can easily infiltrate or otherwise manipulate them. When the true leaders of the Red Brigades were arrested, for example, the man who failed to communicate a warning to them soon took charge, militarized the organization, and then orchestrated the kidnapping and assassination of Prime Minister Aldo Moro in 1978. According to Willan, this man, Mario Moretti, was working for Italian and US intelligence services and made frequent trips to the CIA station in Paris. The history of the strategy of tension in Italy shows how violence is drip-fed to a public that comes to crave security, and how the strict hierarchy of terrorist organizations obscures the real leaders in a way that keeps them above suspicion, either from other members or the public.

We remember journalists, such as Claire Sterling in *Terror Network*,[1] who had themselves been fed disinformation and then conditioned us into thinking that the Italian Red Brigade

---

[1] For a refutation see Edward Herman, *Real Terror Network* (Boston, 1982).

members were who they said they were—with no connections to the CIA, Italian military intelligence, and the P2 Masonic lodge. Now we read the testimony of none other than the former head of Italian military counter-intelligence, General Gianadelio Maletti, who affirms that Americans used false-flag operations, deploying right-wing terrorists trained at a clandestine NATO base in Sardinia, under left-wing guises. He testified that Americans would "do anything to stop Italy from sliding to the left"[1] in the ongoing trial for the 1969 bombing of a bank on Milan's Piazza Fontana that marked the advent of the strategy of tension by killing sixteen and wounding many more. We also remember arching our eyebrows when Vice President George Herbert Walker Bush, himself a member of the semisecret Skull and Bones society, spent the week of Reagan's first inauguration with Lucio Gelli, the P2's master conspirator and, like Reagan, a Knight of Malta who was implicated so deeply in these intrigues in all accounts we have read on the subject.[2] We are sure someone will find the remaining invisible ink on his fingers because, among other reasons, we remember that Gelli was slated for execution by Italian partisans for his Nazi collaboration but escaped via collaboration with the US Army Counter Intelligence Corps.

---

[1] Philip Willan, "Terrorists 'helped by CIA' to stop rise of left in Italy," *The Guardian*, March 26, 2001.
[2] In addition to Willan, see Richard Drake, *The Aldo Moro Murder Case* (Cambridge, 1995); Jean-François Brozzu-Gentile, *L'Affaire Gladio* (Paris, 1994); Jean-Louis Fournel "L'Italie face aux 'années de plomb,'" *Le Monde diplomatique* January 1988.

When Italian police raided Gelli's villa in 1981, they found lists of societies affiliated with P2, which included Opus Dei, the secretive Catholic sect that has found favor with Pope John Paul II. These were groups that called for weekly self-flagellation and daily wearing of spiked chains that cut into the flesh because of their overtly fascistic tendencies. We wonder when someone will investigate the possible tie between convicted FBI spy Robert Hanssen and his former boss Louis Freeh who reportedly sends his son to an Opus Dei school. Although Opus Dei denies it, reports have surfaced that former FBI Director Freeh, and Supreme Court Justices Antonin Scalia and Clarence Thomas are members. Scalia's wife reportedly attends Opus Dei functions; Hanssen, Scalia, and Freeh all worshipped at the same church in Virginia.[1]

4.

We may never know if the al-Qaeda skyjacking teams were infiltrated or not, although Mossad expert Thomas Gordon writes that al-Qaeda operations in the United States were in fact infiltrated. We have every reason to suspect that on American Airlines flight 11, one passenger shot another, as reported by UPI

---

[1] Catharine Henningsen, "Luminous Fallibility: Spies, Spooks and the Catholic Church?" taconline.org, April 2001.

based on an FAA memo. The author of the story revealed that the man who was shot, Daniel Lewin, was a member of the Israeli anti-terror group that "pursues terrorists beyond Israel's borders."[1] Our suspicions are aroused when we hear suggestions in *Newsweek* and elsewhere that three terrorists listed addresses on Pensacola Naval Air Station on their drivers' licenses. Were they infiltrators? Did they learn how to fly there? If not, what were they doing there?

Florida Senator Bill Nelson wanted to know in a press release, before he hushed up on the subject. Did any of the skyjackers, such as Atta, receive specialized training, as a high-ranking Pentagon official told *Newsweek*, at the Air War College in Montgomery, Alabama?[2] Did Mohammad Atta associate with ex-Iran-Contra operatives in Venice Beach, Florida while taking flight training?

Dan Hopsicker's video *Mohammed Atta and the Venice Flying Circus* (From the Wilderness, 2002) makes it clear that Atta was sending e-mail to defense contractor Virtual Prototype and that Huffman Aviation owner Rudi Dekkers had more suspicious connections than your run-of-the-mill flight school operator. Hopsicker takes his title from the fact that a famous circus runs its clown school in Venice, where it also trains CIA agents in slight of hand maneuvers. The Joint Inquiry Committee must

---

[1] UnansweredQuestions.Org transcript of "9-11 and the Public Safety: Seeking Answers and Accountability," June 9, 2002 press conference, 47.
[2] George Wehrfritz, et. al., "Alleged Hijackers May Have Trained at U.S. Bases," *Newsweek*, September 15, 2001.

look into Hopsicker's eyewitness accounts that place Atta and other skyjackers in Venice the month and week before 9-11, which is at odds with the government timeline, as if an attempt were being made to airbrush their presence out of the town.

Hopsicker presents what he calls "anomalous evidence" regarding Richard Boehlke, who financed Huffman Aviation and Flair (Florida Air) for Dekkers, suspiciously sinking money into dubious projects that were, according to locals, protected from police inspection by intelligence agencies. Boehlke may become central to the investigation if it follows the money. We also want to know more about the man, well known to investigators, who recruited suicide pilots in Germany for Huffman Aviation. What were this man's connections and allegiances?

We have more questions for the Joint Inquiry investigation. Were Israeli spies living near by Atta in Florida, keeping a close eye on the future skyjackers? Was the former Iraqi soldier who is suspected by many to be third man in the Oklahoma City bombing and one of the infamous "others unknown,"[1] as former State Department terrorism chief Larry Johnson says,[2] later allowed to work at Logan Airport?

We doubt these questions will be honestly answered by the Congressional Joint Inquiry Committee or a blue-ribbon commission, should one be appointed. To all those who want to

---

[1] Stephen Jones, *Others Unknown* (New York, 2001).
[2] Interview with Bill O'Reilly, Fox News, May 7.

understand the nature of these operations, we recommend the following three sentences:

A constant feature of right-wing bombings has been the deliberate muddying of the waters by the representatives of the Italian secret services. On occasion, the secret services have had prior knowledge of terrorist attacks but have done nothing to prevent them; they have protected from prosecution people suspected of involvement in terrorism; and they have laid false trails for investigating magistrates. Repeated scandals have prompted repeated attempts at reform and the removal of so-called 'deviant' elements, but the secret services have remained true to their central objective, even when this has involved complicity with terrorists.[1]

Sanguinetti was in Milan at the time of the Piazza Fontana bombing and saw the event for what it was in a tract entitled *Is the Reichstag Burning?*, an allusion to the February 1933 baiting of a Dutch anarchist for setting fire to the parliament building in Berlin, which international investigators found to be a Nazi provocation. Hitler used the incident to force President Hindenburg's hand in issuing a decree suspending most civil and political liberties. The Dutchman who was erroneously blamed for this false-flag operation was tried and executed. Nazis swept the ensuing elections.

The distinction made by Sanguinetti, namely that terror can be for defense as well as offense, in other words, used for defensive purposes by the state, should be applied to all terrorist

---

[1] Willan, *Puppetmasters*, 14.

44

acts prior to other distinctions, such as international and domestic terrorism. Are we dealing with a fringe group or a state? That is the fundamental question because it more accurately identifies the enemy than the international-domestic distinction that is blurred by of many considerations, such as alliances and blowback.[1] Numerous examples, from the low intensity warfare operations conducted in Central and South America—Operation Condor comes to mind[2]—demonstrate the direct use of terrorism by the state, that is, open displays of violence by the state or paramilitary organizations acting on its behalf terrorize the public into subordination. The Italian example shows how defensive terrorism is often accomplished indirectly, under a false flag, but always in a way designed to make citizens feel more dependent on the state. To mention another example, we read about the case of a purported anarchist, Gianfranco Bertoli, who was actually military intelligence informant Negro, a man not with left- but right-wing sympathies. He killed four and injured forty-five in 1973 with a bomb aimed at a minister.[3] Renegades do seek absurd military goals for offensive, in both noun and adjective senses of the word, ends. It would be naïve, however, to ignore the many terrorist events perpetrated for *raisons d'état*.

---

[1] Statesmen who deny that al-Qaeda members comprised U.S. allies in the liberation of Afghanistan from Soviet occupation and again allies in Kosovo are either unaware or misinforming the public.

[2] Daniel Brandt, "Operation Condor: Ask the DEA," Namebase Newsline http://www.pir.org.

[3] Philip Willan, *The Guardian*, March 26, 2001.

5.

The word *terror* is most readily traced to the French Revolution, which is an excellent example of the despotic powers of a modern nation-state. Terrorist tactics were used by Girondins against Jacobins, as when young Charlotte Corday assassinated the great Marat in his home. These tactics justified the Jacobin dictatorship's defense of the revolution against real and imaginary traitors and counter-revolutionaries. It was always in defense of the revolution that executions of thousands were justified by Robespierre and his fellow Jacobins on the Committee of Public Safety, centered in Paris.

This was the official Terror with its celebrity trials and executions, the great example being Marie-Antoinette, who was described as audacious and insolent right up to the moment she climbed the scaffold. The terrorists, as they were called, wanted more terror. She merely trembled and her legs buckled as the executioner put her head in the guillotine. The Terror also took hold in areas of Federal Revolt, where the real massacres happened, and in other parts of France policed by civilian revolutionary armies.

The sans-culottes, so called because they wore workers' trousers rather than aristocratic knee-breeches, comprised these armies and forced the Convention to proclaim the Terror on September 5, 1793. The revolutionary armies hated the wealthy and did with them as they pleased. By October, the Committee of Public Safety was given dictatorial powers and ordered the sans-culottes disbanded. Jacobin dictatorship made great strides, then stumbled and lost support. The sans-culottes would rise in Germinal and Prairial, revolts that take their name from the months of the revolutionary calendar, Prairial being their last-gasp storming of the Convention, easily co-opted then suppressed, and the final curtain call for workers during the French Revolution. Robespierre, Saint-Just, and Couthon, who had been deposed in a coup on 9 Thermidor, were released from prison and taken by supporters to Hôtel de Ville where they were later recaptured. On 10 Thermidor the revolutionary Jacobin dictators were themselves guillotined without trial on Place de Grèves.

If the first modern conception of terrorism is defensive, that is in defense of the French Revolution, its origins have a more offensive character and go back to the assassination of a tyrant in the name of justice in Antiquity, as when Marcus Junius Brutus and others conspired against Julius Cæsar on the Ides of March, 44 B.C. Twenty-three stab wounds were found on the body of the man who, after defeating Pompey in 45, was made dictator for life. Here is Plutarch's account of the killing of the man who would be king:

Tillius, laying hold of his robe with both hands, pulled it down from his neck, which was the signal for the assault. Casca gave him the first cut in the neck, neither mortal nor dangerous, as if coming from one who at the beginning of such a bold action was very disturbed. immediately turned and grabbed the dagger and kept hold of it. Both men yelled: He that received the blow in Latin, "Vile Casca, what does this mean," and he that gave it in Greek, to his brother, "Brother, help!" Those who were not privy to the design were astonished and dared not assist Cæsar, or run, or so much as say a word. Those who came prepared for the business enclosed him on every side, naked daggers in hand. Whichever way he turned, Cæsar saw swords leveled at his face and eyes. He was encompassed like an ensnared wild beast. It had been agreed that they should each make a thrust and flesh themselves with his blood. Brutus also gave him a stab in the groin. Some say he fought and resisted all the rest, shifting his body to avoid the blows, calling out for help, but when he saw Brutus's sword drawn, Cæsar covered his face with his robe and submitted, letting himself fall, whether by chance or pushed, at the foot of Pompey's statue, which was wetted with his blood. Pompey himself seemed to have presided over the revenge done upon his adversary, who lay there at his feet, and breathed out his soul through his wounds, for they say he received three and twenty. And the conspirators themselves were wounded by each other although they had leveled their blows at the same person.[1]

The terrifying Islamic terrorist group known to Westerners of the Middle Ages, much the way al-Qaeda is to us, was called the Assassins—this is true whether or not we consider assassination to be a terrorist tactic (we do) and legends of the first Old Man, Hassan Sabbah, to be true (we do not). Marco Polo tells us about a fortified valley between two mountains

---

[1] Plutarch, *Lives of Illustrious Men* (New York, n.d.), vol. II, 552.

growing all varieties of fruit and watered with wine, milk, and honey, possibly the main Assassin stronghold of Alamut. Its palaces hosted dancers and musicians where young men were drugged and became convinced they were in paradise. When again drugged and taken to the Old Man's court, they risked anything to be able to return.[1] Like al-Qaeda and Palestinian suicide bombers, Nizaris welcomed death during the assassination.

Old Man Hassan hailed from western Persia where he grew up in a Twelver Shia family before converting to Ismailism, which recognized only seven prophets, the last being Ismail. In 1078, Hassan went to Cairo and received permission to spread Ismaili gospel in Persia on the condition that he support the caliph's son, Nizar, in a future succession. This is how the Nizaris or Assassins were born; they would become a secret band of hashish-eating Moslems that killed Christian leaders, such as Conrad of Montferrat, Prince of Tyre and King of Jerusalem, in the twelfth and thirteenth century Crusades. It was through them that the word *assassin* entered French and English.

We pause here because although the Assassins began with offensive moves against fellow Arabs and Moslems, drawing ire upon fellow Ismailis and spreading disunity with this flawed tactic, they nonetheless have an arguably defensive quality given who was invading whom with regard to Crusaders. Their

---

[1] David Annan, "The Assassins and the Knights Templar," in Norman MacKenzie, *Secret Societies* (New York, 1967), 106–117.

assassinations were nonetheless the offensive form of terrorism because, as with Montferrat, they attacked the established power, which itself had invaded with massacre tactics and what was arguably offensive terror. The Mongol general Hulagu showed how weak Assassin defenses were by razing fortress after fortress, even the strategically situated one on the mountainside at Alamut. This is depicted concisely in a few stylish pages by Amin Maalouf in his novel *Samarkand*.[1]

The modern conception of offensive terrorism, which, with the notable exceptions of political assassinations and the Assassins, is what concerns us, dates to the nineteenth century Russian populist movement, Narodniki, and its secret organization, the People's Will, comprising experienced revolutionaries who supported assassinations against despots, but condemned them in democracies. People's Will terrorists took shots at Tsar Alexander II when he went for walks, they put mines in royal trains, they exploded dynamite under the dining room of the royal palace. The Tsar was finally killed on March 1, 1881 when Ignaty Grinevitsky threw the second bomb into the royal coach, although the regime remained essentially the same. Our favorite account of People's Will is Yuri Trifonov's *The Impatient Ones* because he captures the sense of infallibility and directness that harnessed the chariot of history: "We shall not waste time as we used to on such trifles as the killing of

---

[1] Amin Maalouf, *Samarkand* (New York, 1998), 150–2.

Kropotkin[1] and Mezentsev. We shall go for the main target—the czar!"[2]

The Socialist Revolutionaries in Russia also used assassinations as a weapon in their arsenal as a way to incite the masses, but it was clear that this tactic would not attain success. As if responding to one of Sanguinetti's early examples of state terror, *Entangled in Terror* by Anna Giefman tries to rehabilitate one of the czar's provocateurs, the legendary Evno Azef.[3]

Giefman uses slippery arguments such as the notion that all spies and infiltrators were called provocateurs at that time; she admits and then conveniently discounts the fact that this Okhrana agent committed terrorist acts for the Socialist Revolutionaries. We can only speculate on Azef's motives, and it's hard to believe anyone involved in the affair, but we wouldn't discredit Boris Savinkov's memoirs as easily as Geifman—he had first hand knowledge and he was shown more evidence later.[4]

It seems probable that the Okhrana conspired with bombers to justify shakedowns. The Okhrana's motive was simple—it would make it look like the Okhrana was needed more than ever to restore law and order, which Geifman concedes.

Anarchists attained perhaps the most acclaim as terrorists and theoreticians who advocated terror—Bakunin, Kropotkin, Nechaev in Russia; Henry, Ravachol, Vailland in France; or the

---

[1] Not a reference to the anarchist, but to a government official.
[2] Yuri Trifonov, *The Impatient Ones* (Moscow, 1978), 197.
[3] Anna Giefman, *Entangled in Terror* (Wilmington, 2000), passim.
[4] Boris Savinkov, *Souvenirs d'un terroriste* (Paris, 1982).

Italian Enrico Malatesta, who invented the expression "propaganda by the deed." The theory behind this expression was developed before and after Malatesta by the French physician Paul Brousse, who meant by it demonstrations, insurrections, and other collective actions along the lines of the Paris Commune, not the concept of individual assassination and terror that would come to be associated with the expression.[1] Propaganda by the deed, between 1893 and 1901, claimed French President Carnot, Spanish Prime Minister Cánovas, Austria-Hungarian Empress Elizabeth, Italian King Umberto, and US President McKinley. No government was threatened by these assassinations as they only drew active support from a minority.

The First World War was touched off by the assassination of Arch-Duke Franz Ferdinand in Sarajevo by a Serb patriot. But after the war, terrorism's obvious form came from the Soviet Union, which defended the revolution with War Communism and institution of a police state. Offensive terror was more localized, as in Ireland, or a tactic favored by fascists such as Mussolini in Italy and Hitler in Germany who sought a monopoly of power and used terror against autonomous institutions and the opposition. On the other hand, many Western communists, with Marx, were against terrorism and for collective violence on a class-war basis that drew on the Paris Commune as a model for urban insurrection. Fascists used terror to gain and defend their

---

[1]   Paul Avrich, *Anarchist Portraits* (Princeton, 1988), 243.

power, which is to say their cause. On their rise, fascists deployed offensive terror to take control of the state and then followed with defensive terror. As William Shirer put it early on, in his *Berlin Diary* entry of September 27, 1934: "...the shadow of Nazi fanaticism, sadism, persecution, regimentation, terror, brutality, suppression, militarism, and preparation for war has hung over all our lives, like a dark, brooding cloud that never clears." Examples of Nazi terror include Kristellnacht in 1938 and the looting of Jewish businesses in Germany, the burning of synagogues, the murders and deportations of twenty thousand Jews to concentration camps with hints about the Final Solution.

In Vietnam, terrorism was deployed in cities and in the countryside by the National Front of Liberation to kill officials and police. The CIA was guilty of the same tactics. Dirty tricks began in 1954 to overthrow the government of North Vietnam and were later escalated in the Phoenix Program, "under which forty thousand Vietnamese local and municipal leaders were assassinated."[1] In Vietnam, state terror suffered a rare defeat. The Algerian liberation movement, which sought to intimidate the population while killing agents of colonialism, served as a rare and only nominally successful model and a pole of support for urban terrorism when it gained independence from France in 1962. Palestinian, Basque, Irish—these liberation movements all

---

[1] Jonathan Vankin and John Whalen, *The Seventy Greatest Conspiracies of All Time* (New York, 1995), 476.

used terror largely for its psychological effects, with limited effectiveness.

The international terrorism we confront now was born in 1968 with the skyjacking by the Popular Front for the Liberation of Palestine of an El Al jetliner en route from Rome to London. The passengers and crew were detained for weeks in Algiers; the perpetrators were apprehended and then freed. Skyjacking attacks, as they were rightly called at the time to distinguish them from highway robbery, on Israeli commercial airliners and their offices continued for decades with various levels of support from Algeria, Iraq, Syria, Libya, Lebanon, Uganda, Somalia, and Kuwait.

Until the recent wave of suicide bombings, Israeli airlines and defense forces had the upper hand on Palestinian terrorism. We have in mind such startling successes as Yani Netanyahu's 1976 raid on Entebbe and the forestallment of assassination attempts in foreign countries. On the subject of assassinations, we share Barry Chamish's suspicions about the assassination of Rabin, and likewise suspect an inside job. Chamish reports that the May 27, 2002 fire in the Israeli embassy in Paris was a convenience designed to destroy evidence: "Now history will never know the tawdry crimes of the French government against Israel, nor will Shimon Peres' central role in these crimes, including the Rabin assassination, be proven in time for his ever more likely upcoming trials. From here on until forever, the French government's collusion with Peres on the Golan Heights, the murder of Paris Ambassador Eliahu Ben Elissar, the backing of PFLP terror attacks, the secret talks with the Vatican, including negotiations between Peres' rabbis Rosen and Melchoir with French Cardinal Lustinger to divvy up Jerusalem, all this and more will never be provable in a court of law or scholarship." We quote Chamish even though we cannot verify his claims as to what was inside the embassy because of what he says about Paris. As implausible as it sounds for France to back the Popular Front for the Liberation of Palestine terror attacks, we recall that CIA headquarters in Paris served as a conduit for a PLO weapons deal with the Red Brigades.[1]

Israel, with US backing, still has the upper hand as it did when it allowed the Sabra and Shatilla massacres. The 1992 Palestinian intifadah pitted pipe bombs and knives against guns and tank attacks. The rare car bomb was mostly directed against the military; not more than a few hundred people were killed, most of them Palestinian. The suicide attacks associated with the second intifadah are deadly disruptions of daily life, terrifying reminders of Palestinian claims, not a real military threat to the entire state of Israel. Sharon terrorizes the terrorists and many innocents by pitting the military against civilians. Israel's defensive solution in 2002 appears to be to try to provoke a Palestinian civil war by humiliating Arafat and destroying the

---

[1] Philip Willan, *Puppetmasters* (London, 1991), 196–197.

PLO, in addition to the habitual killing of women and children who happen to be in the way.

The direct defensive attacks also serve as a diversion from conflicts between ultraorthodox and secular Jews, but if we are to believe critics in Israel, such as Professor Baruch Kimmerling, the right-wing is intent on "partial or nearly complete ethnic cleansing of the Arabs in the 'Land of Israel.'"[1]

As mentioned in the preface regarding the attack in 2002,[2] Israel has engaged in cross-border assassinations, such as the retaliation in 1973 that liquidated three leaders. In its use of this tactic, Israel is not alone. During the early sixties, the CIA established a division codenamed ZR/RIFLE to train assassins using dart guns, guns with magnetic bullets, snake venom, poison-coated minibombs, Walther PPKS .22s with silencers and .44 magnums without, land mines the size of tea bags, LSD-laced cough drops, fléchettes loaded with sodium cyanide, canisters of poison gas, and all the other devices worthy of novels by Fleming or Le Carré rather than Castro, for whom they were often intended. The September 1976 car-bomb assassination of former Chilean ambassador Orlando Letelier and his American associate Ronni Moffitt in Washington by someone who had long ties to the CIA and received only a few years in prison is one indication among so many that the state gets who it wants and gets away

---

[1] Baruch Kimmerling, "I Accuse" *Kol Ha'Ir*, February 1, 2002.
[2] Cf., 29–30.

with it.[1]   The leftist terrorism associated with political movements—November 17 in Greece, named after the student riots in 1973 that deposed the generals; the Röte Armee Fraktion, in Germany better knows as the Baader-Meinhof gang, completely rounded-up by 1983; and the Red Brigades in Italy, which we discussed in other sections, to mention a few examples—were deadly irritants when they were authentically offensive forms of terrorism. They didn't threaten the established order so much as inadvertently support it because terrorism is a flawed means to win over people of good will to any movement.

6.

The playbook of power routinely draws on a nineteenth century strategist, the Prussian General Carl von Clausewitz whose most famous conception, often misused, is that war is "the simple continuation of politics by other means." This is an axiom

---

[1]   See the National Security Archive's Chile Documentation Project directed by Peter Kornbluh for information about the assassination of Letelier and the CIA's ties to the Chilean secret police, the DINA. The project is also enlightening in regard to the CIA's use of black propaganda, bribery, payoffs, funding of a right-wing paper and a right-wing economic institute, creation of arrest lists, and liaison of security police and security forces. Nixon's coup-plotting is revealed in another, ominously titled document provided by the project,"Alleged Assassination Plots Involving Foreign Leaders," An Interim Report of the Select Committee to Study Governmental Operations with respect to Intelligence Activities, United States Senate, November 20, 1975.

to live by in Washington where directives are sent to assassination teams that otherwise deal drugs and illegally sell arms around the world.[1]

Clausewitz is less well known for his distinction between absolute war and real war. The former comprises a theory of war without limits in which rivals push violence to extreme limits. This was extrapolated by German General Erich Ludendorff in his strategy of total war, which he deployed in the First World War in an eponymous and ill-fated offensive on the Western Front and by using chemical gas and bombing cities. Clausewitz's latter conception, real war, acknowledges that circumstances and chance often determine the course of events and put constraints on what is theoretically the goal of total annihilation of the enemy.

Our current statesmen, and their terrorist rivals, seemed capable of keeping the two concepts of absolute war and real war in mind at the same time. The terrorists pushed the limits of violence, true to absolute war, and deployed new military technology against civilians. Surprise, as with the skyjacking, always implies stratagem in the context of real war. To invade Afghanistan as the first stage in an absolute war on terrorism, circumstances had to ripen; a blind eye stratagem, a costly one, needed to be deployed on a scale matching the state's belligerent ambitions. Misdirection may have been at work on several fronts,

---

[1] Christic Institute, *Inside the Shadow Government* (Washington, 1988), 205-214.

but as with past conflicts, information dominance, as the Pentagon calls it, shifting circumstances, and diversions prevented ruses from finding their way to the public's attention.

Clausewitz wrote, "to begin with defense and end with offense fully corresponds to the natural course of war." This statement lays bare a prime rationale for the defensive use of terror in general, and in particular, the early sixties plans for Operation Northwoods, to mention a fairly recent American example. Formulated and approved by the Joint Chiefs, the plan envisioned using staged terror in the United States as a pretext to invade Cuba.

Documents unearthed by NSA expert James Bamford, whose understated prose slyly masks his alarming revelations, reveal that the military top brass gave its collective written approval to orchestrate murders, bombings, and skyjackings in the United States, in Castro's name: "Exploding a few plastic bombs in carefully chosen spots, the arrest of Cuban agents and the release of prepared documents substantiating Cuban involvement also would be helpful in projecting the idea of an irresponsible government."[1]

The plans, which were repeatedly presented by the military to the Kennedy Administration, envisioned a rash of false terror attacks in Miami and Washington, and even a few plots worthy of Hollywood. For example, the chiefs would explode the first

---

[1] Bamford, *Body of Secrets*, 85.

rocket to orbit the earth, with John Glenn inside, and blame it on Cuban electronic interference. There were plans to stage the bombing of a drone that was simulating a passenger airline, orchestrated so that the International Civil Aviation Organization notification would make the incident seem authentic.

Those who have cultivated historical consciousness know better than to assume the best in people. Conspiratorial plans play a part in most, if not all, historical events. The admirals and generals under Joint Chiefs Chairman Lyman Lemnitzer knew their history and planned to reenact the 1898 explosion, possibly staged by the United States, of the battleship Maine[1] in the Havana harbor that set the Spanish-American War ablaze. The sixties-era generals and admirals planned to "blow up a U.S. ship in Guantanamo Bay and blame Cuba."

The generals would foment riots by Cubans in front of the base while provocateurs fired weapons and set off bombs. The chiefs planned what would look like Cuban air raids into the Dominican Republic, which would then request assistance from the United States. The US military *did* make provocative flights over Cuba with the hope that an incident would occur to justify war. Castro was too wise a fish to snap at this lure.

With revelations like Operation Northwoods in mind, any adult analysis of 9-11 would be incomplete without careful consideration of the state-terror thesis, which is to say that the

---

[1]   As newspaper magnate William Randolph Hearst said at the time, "You provide me with the pictures and I'll provide you the war."

state indirectly attacked its citizens so as to go on the offensive. We will demonstrate motive, opportunity, evidence of advance knowledge, and negligence. Congress probably will not explore these aspects of 9-11 in its Joint Inquiry Committee. They may ignore them or otherwise cover them up because they're afraid of what they will find, although we hope they prove us wrong.

7.

The September 9 al-Qaeda killing of the Lion, the Northern Alliance Defense Minister Ahmad Shah Masoud, by suicide assassins posing as friendly journalists caught many people, especially the victim, by surprise. The video man wore a battery belt bomb that killed Masoud when shrapnel punctured his heart.[1] This was another tactical victory for Osama bin Laden, one that strengthened his relations with the Taliban. We now hear of more outlandish schemes by bin Laden, such as training terrorists on mock golf courses to storm tournament crowds with machine guns and mow them down like grass on the green. Who would've imagined such a surprise attack? Reality comprises, we're reminded, the revealed and the concealed.

---

[1]   n.a., "The Lion Clawed," *Economist*, September 15, 2001, 50.

We take great pleasure when the concealed is revealed, when what is hidden becomes known and prevented. We derived no pleasure, however, in the prospect that the skyjacked airplane missiles were the result of state action and inaction. We were reminded in part of the *Lusitania* fiasco and the way the government and news organizations either failed to report or minimized the warnings, which were published in 1915 in *New York Times* advertisements by Germany when it began unrestricted U-boat bombing. The British passenger liner *Lusitania*, sailing from New York, nonetheless crossed the Atlantic with munitions, had no escort, and continued on course, directly toward the German blockade, despite recent U-boat attacks and sightings in the area where it was destroyed.

This human catastrophe, which should have been prevented, eventually turned the tide of American public opinion, although at first there was widespread resentment against the British use of US citizens as "human shields" for munitions shipments. The attack on the liner was in fact used in 1917 as part of the argument justifying US entry into the First World War and troops chanted the ship's name as they marched into battle.

President Wilson, under the signature of Secretary of State William Jennings Bryan, sent a revealing letter to the German ambassador after a German submarine torpedoed the luxurious and immense Cunard liner. More than 1,100 passengers, including 124 Americans, went down with the ship off the Irish coast. The list of previous attacks recounted in the letter, along with Germany's high-profile warning, reveal how risky it was to send a passenger across the Atlantic.

In view of recent acts of the German authorities in violation of American rights on the high seas which culminated in the torpedoing and sinking of the British steamship Lusitania on May 7, 1915, by which over 100 American citizens lost their lives, it is clearly wise and desirable that the Government of the United States and the Imperial German Government should come to a clear and full understanding as to the grave situation which has resulted.

The sinking of the British passenger steamer Falaba by a German submarine on March 28, through which Leon C. Thrasher, an American citizen, was drowned; the attack on April 28 on the American vessel Cushing by a German aeroplane; the torpedoing on May 1 of the American vessel Gulflight by a German submarine, as a result of which two or more American citizens met their death and, finally, the torpedoing and sinking of the steamship Lusitania, constitute a series of events which the Government of the United States has observed with growing concern, distress, and amazement.

...The Government of the United States has been apprised that the Imperial German Government considered themselves to be obliged by the extraordinary circumstances of the present war and the measures adopted by their adversaries in seeking to cut Germany off from all commerce, to adopt methods of retaliation which go much beyond the ordinary methods of warfare at sea, in the proclamation of a war zone from which they have warned neutral ships to keep away. This Government has already taken occasion to

inform the Imperial German Government that it cannot admit the adoption
of such measures or such a warning of danger to operate as in any degree an
abbreviation of the rights of American shipmasters or of American citizens
bound on lawful errands as passengers on merchant ships of belligerent
nationality; and that it must hold the Imperial German Government to a
strict accountability for any infringement of those rights, intentional or
incidental.... [1]

The point here is that the warnings and previous attacks, along with the ghastly poison gas attack by Germany on the Western front in April 1917, should have prevented the ship from sailing, at least with civilian passengers and not without escorts. As was the case with the Bush administration in the wake of the September 2001 attacks, the British government was very reluctant to conduct an investigation into what happened and still keeps records on it sealed.

In the early seventies, British journalist Colin Simpson published *The Lusitania*,[2] which made the sensational claim that Winston Churchill, then head of the British Admiralty, intentionally sent the vessel into harms way to involve the United States in the war. Patrick Beesly, a specialist in British naval intelligence, supports this claim in *Room 40: British Naval Intelligence 1914–18*, although other historians—naïve perhaps, or biased, or

---

[1] United States, *Foreign Relations of the United States* (Washington, D.C., 1915), supplement, 393.
[2] Colin Simpson, *Lusitania* (New York, 1983).

both, but not without their justifications—doubt Churchill would act with such bad intentions.

Beesly, however, points out, "The very unsatisfactory nature of the official enquiry held in June 1915 and the refusal then, and for the next sixty-six years, of the British authorities to disclose all the information in their possession, has only succeeded in fueling suspicions ... German and American records are also remarkable for the absence of certain papers which once existed but which can no longer, apparently, be produced." Beesly goes on to say he was "reluctantly driven to the conclusion that there *was* a conspiracy to deliberately put the *Lusitania* at risk in the hopes that even an abortive attack on her would bring the United States into the war. Such a conspiracy could not have been put into effect without Winston Churchill's express permission and approval."[1]

Simpson's revisionist history focuses on the meeting of May 5, 1917 when the decision was made to call the passenger liner's escort, the HMS Juno, back to port without telling the *Lusitania*'s captain his ship was alone. The diary of the meeting suspiciously trails off and no one really knows who made the decision. Simpson draws on Lieutenant Commander Kenworthy, who left the room to express his revulsion for what was taking

---

[1] Patrick Beesly, *Room 40 British Naval Intelligence 1914–1918* (New York, 1982), 122.

place. Kenworthy claims that he had been commissioned by Churchill to write a report on the political repercussions of a German attack on a passenger vessel. Churchill, for his part, has a degree of plausible deniability—after the meeting he had lunch with his wife and then went to Waterloo Station in the first leg of a trip to France for a naval convention that would bring Italy into the war on the Allied side.

Churchill's arguments, when responding to questions in the House of Commons and in later essays, were: 1) British naval superiority was so great that no injury would be brought upon British commerce by the first German submarine campaign, 2) he thought German warnings were bluffs, 3) he thought the *Lusitania* could outrun U-boats or that ramming orders and the advent of the Q-ship would deter attack, and 4) with few exceptions, the navy did not and could not be expected to provide escorts to commercial ships, (although this contradicts the long British use of convoys to protect merchant ships against France and others).[1]

The record of recent successful U-boat attacks, presented in Wilson's letter to the German ambassador, demonstrates the folly of Churchill's first and second arguments. As for the third argument, which comes in two parts, the maneuverability of smaller, hidden vessels made it quite possible for U-boats to get within range of the much larger passenger ships and Churchill

---

[1] Archer Jones, *The Art of War in the Western World* (Oxford, 1989), 467.

knew this. Strategists contemplating war-time scenarios must consider the worst possible case, which, according to an eyewitness, Churchill had done for repugnantly cynical ends. Prior to nuclear deterrence, and even then, one could never rely on the enemy to resist attack. As for the much debated escort question, the fact remains that the captain of the *Lusitania* was told that he would have an escort before he sailed, told by the senior British naval officer in New York the night before he left and never told otherwise. The crucial escort was called off in the May 5 Admiralty meeting. Without a military ship with a hydrophone to track a moving submarine and depth charges to launch a preemptive attack, merchant ships were highly vulnerable. The risk was so readily apparent that the ship's captain was told to throw the weighted diplomatic sack overboard if attacked. Furthermore, he was told as he received his orders that a US ship had just been attacked by U-boat in the Irish Sea.

More attacks followed. On May 5, the same day as the disputed meeting in the map room, a U-boat sank the schooner *Earl of Lathom* off Kinsale and unsuccessfully attacked the British steamer *Cayo Romano* off Queenstown, Ireland. A warning was issued from the navy base on the coast that U-boats were in the area, but no escort was dispatched from London. The next day, cargo ships *Candidate* and *Centurion* were sunk by a U-boat in the entrance to Saint George's Channel. The Admiralty in London withheld information about the *Candidate* sinking from the navy base in Queenstown for twenty-four hours. The *Lusitania* was torpedoed on May 7, 1917 and sank in eighteen minutes. As the theory, supported by no less a historian than Patrick Beesly, goes the Admiralty conspired to guide the *Lusitania* into a trap designed by Churchill who was on the continent with an airtight alibi. If this was the conspirator's intention, they used the Germans to indirectly attack what should have been defended.

8.

The disputed *Lusitania* disaster remains as contentious for historians as Pearl Harbor, which likewise has a Churchill angle and is even more reminiscent of 9-11 for its kamikazi insanity and the ostensibly surprise nature of the attack. The Japanese knew, and al-Qaeda should and probably does know, how nearly impossible it is to defeat a power like the United States in protracted wars, so they attempt knockouts. The preemptive strategy of an assault on the biggest US naval harbor in the Pacific, engineered by Yamamoto, commander-in-chief of the Japanese fleet, called for six aircraft carriers to launch 360 planes on the morning of December 7, 1941.

Yamamoto, a Harvard graduate, was an expert on the United States and knew better, but he went along with the wartime alliance with Germany and devised a plan to destroy the

US Pacific Fleet. Although Admiral Nagumo's fleet killed over two thousand Americans, sunk two battleships, damaged six others, and even sunk three cruisers and three destroyers along with blowing up 261 planes, US carriers were safe at sea. Nagumo, for unknown reasons, failed to launch a search and destroy mission.

Of interest to the 9-11 case, because of the FBI connection, is the fact that historians have known for decades that J. Edgar Hoover withheld information from the White House regarding Japanese plans to attack Pearl Harbor.[1] Hoover was in possession of a German secret service document that pinpointed the harbor as the primary target, but he did not inform President Roosevelt or naval intelligence. Hoover may have been protecting his sources or had other reasons for his reticence, but if he had communicated the fact that Pearl Harbor was a primary target, it seems clear that the two Army radar operators stationed on the northern tip of Oahu who picked up a blip on their oscilloscope, and those they relayed their message to at headquarters, would've reacted differently. The privates operating the mobile radar station actually figured out incoming aircraft were descending on the island like locusts, and they even reported it to their superiors at headquarters.

None of the above is in dispute, what is debatable is whether the largely successful Japanese attack against Pearl

---

[1] John F. Bratzel, and Leslie B. Rout Jr., "Research Note: Pearl Harbor, Micro-dots, and J. Edgar Hoover," *American Historical Review*, volume 87 (1982), 1342-51.

Harbor could have been foiled due to successful and timely breaking of enemy codes, particularly the Winds Code. The words "east winds rain" on the December 4 short-wave radio broadcast from Tokyo, for example, was known to mean "war with the United States," signaling Japanese diplomats to destroy documents, codes, code machines, and prepare for war. The Navy's East Coast Intercept station picked up the "east winds rain" message, and the message was treated with due urgency—then it disappeared. We read in court proceedings that dispatch 7001 was received, but later could not be found by investigators. Then in mirror fashion the Office of US Naval Intelligence ordered Far East stations, except Hawaii which was omitted from the warning, to destroy codes and secret documents.

The detailed Magic intercepts, so-called because of the "magic" security level required to see them, proved advance knowledge of Japanese plans. These intercepts required the Navy cover-up that also extended to the December 5, 1941 "War Alert from the British Admiralty," which remains shamefully secret. Perhaps most damning of all is that on the morning of December 7 both FDR and Navy Secretary Knox were given intercepts that were parsed by the Office of Naval Intelligence as follows: "This means a sunrise attack on Pearl Harbor today." Due to the time difference between Washington and Pearl Harbor, there was still time to issue an alert. Only one was sent, by General George C. Marshall, but it was authorized after such a long and inexplicable delay as to be ineffective. It was sent by commercial telegraph rather than by safer, more efficient military methods.

The "day which will live in infamy," as President Roosevelt called it, finds his hands drenched with blood. Even historians who blame the military men on the scene in Hawaii for being caught off guard, which is dishonest considering all the facts, acknowledge that FDR ignored intelligence and failed to send alerts. The president committed what researchers Henry Clausen and Bruce Lee, in *Pearl Harbor: Final Judgement*, called "contributory negligence." Churchill, on the other hand, claims in *Grand Alliance* that FDR was intent on joining the war and knew full well about enemy plans, although Churchill's November 25, 1941 message to FDR is another one of the documents that remain secret.

The blame game was revealing for the way it scapegoated the admiral and general in charge of defending Pearl Harbor so as to mask the effectiveness of US codebreakers, which, if revealed, would have raised tough questions for FDR. Why didn't he order alerts to the military in Hawaii given the information in his possession? Why did General Douglas MacArthur send false information on the position of the Japanese carrier fleet on three separate occasions in late November and early December? No palatable excuse exists. The proud General George C. Marshall threatened to resign over the findings of a secret report by an Army board that made harsh accusations that he could not refute. He was shamed by lower-ranking officers for lying about when he received intercepts and displaying more loyalty to his leader than his country.

A short quote from the "Top Secret Report of Army Pearl Harbor Board," October 20, 1944, is telling:

Information from informers and other means as to the activities of our potential enemy and their intentions in the negotiations between the United States and Japan was in possession of the State, War and Navy Departments in November and December of 1941. Such agencies had a reasonably complete disclosure of the Japanese plans and intentions, and were in a position to know what were the Japanese potential moves that were scheduled by them against the United States. Therefore, Washington was in possession of essential facts as to the enemy's intentions.

This information showed clearly that war was inevitable and late in November absolutely imminent. It clearly demonstrated the necessity for resorting to every trading act possible to defer the ultimate day of breach of relations to give the Army and Navy time to prepare for the eventualities of war.

The messages actually sent to Hawaii by either the Army or Navy gave only a small fraction of this information. No direction was given to the Hawaiian Department based upon this information except the "Do-Don't" message of November 27, 1941. It would have been possible to have sent safely information, ample for the purpose of orienting the commanders in Hawaii, or positive directives could have been formulated to put the Department on Alert Number 3.

This was not done.

Congress voted to declare war on Japan with only one vote against the measure. Members of later sessions were naturally resentful when historians reminded them that in November 1941, just prior to the attack, Secretary of War Stimson testified that FDR had made a remarkable declaration. Stimson said that the president had told him, "The question was how we should maneuver them into the position of firing the first shot without allowing too much danger to ourselves." This is a clear expression of the president wanting an indirect defensive attack. We will come back to the charge of contributory negligence, which has been superceded by comparative negligence in most courts. Just as Bush is creating the Department of Homeland Security in response to September 11, Pearl Harbor was used by William L. Langer, a historian with the Office of Strategic Services, to argue for more intelligence integration and for creation of the CIA.

Langer would go on to found the Office of the Historian in the CIA and coauthor a study using privileged access to primary source material, on US entry into the Second World War that dishonestly glossed over the intelligence issue. Congress held hearings on the subject in the mid-nineties which along with the research of independent historians, more evidence emerged, such as eyewitness accounts of Roosevelt and Churchill calmly reacting to the event as if both had known in advance. We still don't know what British Prime Minister Winston Churchill told FDR about the planned attack because the files on the subject remain sealed in London.[1]

9.

At Pearl Harbor, America's adversary attacked military targets, which makes Roosevelt's impassive strategy to enter the war somewhat more palatable, if no less cynical, than similar impassivity, similar feigning of incapacity and slowness to act, that appears to have been deployed by the Bush administration last autumn. September 11 was first and foremost a massacre, which is the murder of unresisting humans under cruel circumstances, and one would have to be criminally insane to find pleasure in knowing that the state contributed to the event.

When we cast this displeasing event in the harsh light it deserves and take a penetrating look at it, we can compare it to other massacres in history, such as the Jerusalem massacre in 1099 perpetrated by Christian crusaders who boasted of wading knee-deep in blood. Or the infamous massacre at My Lai—we remember the twisted logic used in the Vietnam War, expressed so eloquently by the US major who said, "It became necessary to destroy the town to save it." It is our assertion that from the

---

[1] See Suggested Reading.

Reign of Terror to the present, massacres have been perpetrated more by states than any other institution or social group and they routinely lie about their role.

Terrorism is massacre, with the accentuated political and psychological objective of spreading fear in the masses. The word *terror* is loaded, it tends to conveniently exclude the political class of nation states. Why? Because it is assumed that statesmen would never act with such ill will?

The word *terror* begs the question why, for what political ends, was the violence carried out. We are with Chomsky when he accepts the US government's definition: "the calculated use of violence or threat of violence to attain goals that are political, religious, or ideological in nature. This is done through intimidation, coercion, or instilling fear."[1] Few people other than anarchists and military historians seem willing to acknowledge the truth about the one institution that has by definition a virtual monopoly on military force, namely the state. This is surprising given the term's ties to the French revolutionary state, mentioned above, and the way Goebbels, whom Hitler made plenipotentiary for total war with vast powers over the civilian population, systematically used the term for propaganda purposes.

The word *massacre* is more clear-cut than *terror*—it tells us that helpless people were killed under atrocious circumstances, such as the bombing of Dresden, which killed 100,000 people in

---

[1] Noam Chomsky, *9–11* (New York, 2001), 90–91.

a city that was not, as Winston Churchill claimed in *Triumph and Tragedy*, a military target. Nor was Hiroshima a legitimate military target as Truman claimed in his radio address after he dropped the bomb. We will not enter the neverending debate over how many people were massacred by Stalin except to describe him as a fascist executioner rivaling Hitler. But even the basic notion that states perpetrate massacres can be obscured by someone like Elliot Abrams, the Reagan administration diplomat who referred to massacres in Latin America not as "killing," but as the "unlawful or arbitrary deprivation of life." We were not surprised to read the report in *The Observer* that Abrams, now with Bush the Younger, gave the nod for the 2002 military coup in Venezuela in which more than a hundred people died.[1]

Unlike the infamous Valentine's Day massacre, most, if not nearly all, massacres in modern history were authored by statesmen—Hitler had his Holocaust, Truman his Hiroshima, H.W. Bush his Gulf massacre, the horrors of which are still not widely known. Bush the Younger now has his massacre at Mazar-i-Sharif, Afghanistan,[2] and as he threatens another massacre in Iraq, we must always remember that the father danced to one

---

[1] Ed Vulliamy, "Venezuela coup linked to Bush team: Specialists in the 'dirty wars' of the Eighties encouraged the plotters who tried to topple President Chavez," *Observer*, April 21, 2002.

[2] Clive Freeman, "Documentary of US 'war crimes' shocks Europe," *Independent*, June 12, 2002; Jonathan Harley, *Lateline*, Australian Broadcasting Corporation, June 19, 2001.

tune with Saddam behind closed doors and sang another to the public.[1]

10.

A link between terrorism and the state is harder to prove than one with massacres; it often requires disclosures for it to emerge from its hiding places, disclosures that remain partially guarded by plausible deniability. The Iran-Contra players still deny their massive military support for Iraq, sponsor of terrorist Abu Nidal, despite all the disclosures by insiders and the banking scandals surrounding the profiteering that went on around this longstanding operation. All of this is documented by *Financial Times* correspondent Alan Freidman in *Spider's Web*,[2] usually with multiple reliable sources, even on the most sensitive points. Who knew that Saudi Arabia, with US approval, convinced Abu Nidal to move from Iraq to a safe haven in Saudi Arabia prior to Operation Desert Storm? He was given a home, an office, and millions of dollars to suspend his terrorist operations.[3]

Proof for the state-massacre thesis, from the firing squad to so-called collateral damage to lethal medical experiments, is

---

[1] Alan Freidman, *Spider's Web* (New York, 1993).
[2] Ibid.
[3] Ibid., 178.

obvious and irrefutable. If states have perpetrated by far the most massacres in the modern era, and if what we think of as terrorism is always a massacre, plus macabre psychological intentions, then we can't exclude any state as a source of terrorism.

George Bush partially acknowledges this when he refers to state-sponsored terrorism in the same breath as his axis of evil. Although he appears more likely to deceive himself than others, perhaps he learned from his father how to tell half a secret to conceal the rest. Always insist that only others practice terrorism and do whatever you need to for the latest investor-driven goal. If the spirit of the American Revolution has diminished to the point that its current leaders would support the massacres in New York and Washington, either directly or indirectly, to manipulate markets and terrorize the population into supporting war, then the United States as we knew it has in fact disappeared and could do so in name as well. United States of Terror would be more accurate.

We promised at the outset to ask pertinent questions. Here is one: Did the administration let its supposed concern for the national interest regarding oil supply, which is in reality a class interest, allow 9-11 to happen as an object in the logic for war? If so, it should resign as Wim Kok's government did in 2002 when the Dutch government's contributory role in the 1995 massacre at Srebrenica was published in an official report. We're reminded of the Parisian lawyer in exile in the Netherlands, as drawn by Camus in *The Fall*, whose settlement of barroom disputes leads him to the judge-penitent position that always pleads guilty as it renders judgment.

We don't expect the president to possess high moral standards like Clamence or the hosts of the international court that judges Serbian leaders. In a euphemism such as Zbigniew Brzezinski's "ideological flexibility,"[1] which he sees as a source of strength for the American Empire, we read the lack of scruples that distinguishes it from Rome and could lead to its premature decline. To this end, we will present evidence that has not been adequately refuted by anyone, much less the supporters of a reckless empire that ceaselessly militarizes and commodifies its subjects, the American Empire to which so many pledge allegiance.

We have examined whether the 9-11 acts were facilitated by several states—United States, Britain, Saudi Arabia, Israel, Iraq, Pakistan, Afghanistan—for various reasons, particularly by the United States as a pretext for war in Afghanistan. If this is the case, and we think it is, it would be even more sinister than the way Hitler staged the seizure of the Gleiwitz Radio Station using people from concentration camps, dressed in Polish uniforms, for false-flag fodder. This was on the eve of September 1, 1939.

Hitler said at the time: "I shall give a propagandist reason for starting the war—never mind if it is plausible or not. The

---

[1] Zbigniew Brzezinski, *Grand Chessboard* (New York, 1997), 7.

victor will not be asked afterwards whether he told the truth. In starting and waging a war, it is not right that matters, but victory."

The historical crime called Operation White was carried out by the SS security service, the Sicherheitsdienst or SD, who posed as Polish guerrillas and stormed a radio station on the German side of the border. They murdered concentration camp prisoners dressed as Poles, the so-called canned goods, and strewed their corpses around the perimeter of the station. German newspapers called it a "signal for a general attack on German territory by Polish guerrillas," and a scale model of the incident with light bulbs and machine gun chatter was used to illustrate the event.[1] The war began with an indirect defensive attack under a false flag.

11.

American citizens watched the gruesome events of September 11 on television, as they happened, and find it impossible to believe that these events were allowed to transpire with precisely this terror-inducing display of crashing planes and crumbling buildings in mind. The "Uniting and Strengthening America by Providing Appropriate Tools Required to Intercept

---

[1] Heinz Höhne, *Order of Death's Hand* (New York, 2001), 260–266.

and Obstruct Terrorism Act of 2001," better known as the USA Patriot Act, which increased police power to combat terrorism[1] as a result of the September attacks, was signed into law on October 26, 2001, virtually unread by legislators facing anthrax attacks. Once again, past is prelude.

Passage of the Anti-Terrorism Act of 1996, which likewise increased police power by provisions such as reviving the guilt by association law that had been used against communists and anarchists in the fifties, succeeded the disturbing events surrounding the Oklahoma City bombings on April 19, 1995— we say *bombings* because we trust eyewitness and seismologist accounts that there were at least two explosions. Congress had rejected many of the act's provisions when they were proposed by President Reagan and Bush the Elder, provisions such as limiting habeas corpus, association as grounds for exclusion or deportation, the ban on supporting lawful activities of groups labeled terrorist, and the use of secret evidence, but an event that has the markings of defensive terrorism created an atmosphere conducive to passage of the draconian law.

By simply connecting the dots in what seems to us to be a highly evident way, we come to Timothy McVeigh's connections with white supremacists in the United States, such as Denis

---

[1] The most troublesome aspect of the act, according to Jennifer Van Bergen in her May 20, 2002 *Truthout* article "The USA Patriot Act was Planned Before 9/11," is the amendment to Section 218 of the Foreign Intelligence Surveillance Act of 1978 allowing surveillance even when primary purpose is not to gather intelligence on foreign powers—agents no longer need probable cause as required by the Fourth Amendment.

Mahon, who reportedly received money from Iraq. Interpol classifies Mahon as a terrorist and he is banned from Canada and Britain, yet he apparently wasn't questioned by the FBI for the Oklahoma City bombings. Certain well-informed authors, such as David Hoffman in *The Oklahoma City Bombing and the Politics of Terror*, suggest that the white separatist community in Elohim City, Oklahoma was a center for government provocateurs just as the KKK was for Hoover's FBI. We liken it to G.K. Chesterton's novel *The Man Who Was Thursday* in which everyone in the group is an agent spying on the others: "I know what you are all of you, from first to last—you are the people in power. You are the police—the great fat, smiling men in blue and buttons."

Investigators eventually checked up on Andreas Strassmeir, another one-term Elohim City resident, a man who attended Bundeswehr Academy in Hanover, Germany and may be a member of a German counterterrorism unit. We found out that he trained members of the Mahon's Aryan Nations and replaced shotguns with assault rifles then exhorted members to perpetuate crimes. "In an effort to fabricate the façade of investigation, the FBI finally contacted John Doe number two suspect Strassmeir by phone in Germany but only after McVeigh's attorney condemned the FBI for not following up on leads," according to Ian Williams Goddard in *Prevailing Winds*. "When Strassmeir was interviewed by the German publication *Report BadenBaden*, he said that when the FBI called him by phone they assured him that

'They would cover for me.'"[1] ATF informant Carol Howe, who was not allowed to testify in McVeigh's trail, has told the press that members of the cross-dressing, bank-robbing Aryan Republican Army also visited Elohim City. They happen to have made an incriminating video about bombing federal buildings prior to the event, but they weren't interviewed, as far as we know, or at least not implicated by the FBI.

We also understand that NBC local affiliate FKOR in Oklahoma City has reported that Tim McVeigh was seen with Hussain al-Hussaini,[2] a former member of Iraq's elite Republican Guard, then living in the city. Eyewitnesses say they saw a Middle Eastern man speeding away from the building prior to the blast, and Paul Bedard writes in the October 29, 2001 *U.S. News and World Report* that defense officials think McVeigh may have been an Iraqi agent because of certain phone numbers in his possession. The FBI and Justice Department have objected to retired FBI Agent Dan Vogel testifying in the state trial of Terry Nichols, possibly because he received affidavits and witness statements placing McVeigh with Middle Eastern men.

According to former State Department terrorism expert Larry Johnson, al-Hussaini left Oklahoma in 1996 or 1997 and went to work for Logan Airport in Boston where two of the

---

[1] Ian Williams Goddard, "Government's Prior Knowledge of the OK City Bombing" *Prevailing Winds* Number Five, 10.
[2] Alternately, Hussein Al-Husseini.

skyjacked planes departed.[1] How could this have happened? Why wasn't this man closely monitored? Johnson suggests that his path, on occasion, crossed that of skyjackers Mohamed Atta, Marwan al-Shehi, and Zacorias Moussaoui. Has history repeated itself in this particular way? Was the same man involved in both attacks?

We have attempted to formulate a fairly precise reasoning on questions that hinge on the fact that McVeigh was convicted of conspiring to use a weapon of mass destruction based on a single bomb theory. This event supports the state-terror thesis because abundant evidence backs the contention that the state attacked itself under the false flag of militias, a clear example of defensive terrorism. We are interested in the tactic of blaming a lone wolf like Oswald or a couple of them, like McVeigh and Nichols, when evidence suggests many others were involved. We suspect this to be the case with the Amerithrax attacks subsequent to 9-11.

In McVeigh's trial the government didn't produce any witnesses that placed him at the scene of the crime, because if they had, the witnesses would have acknowledged that he was in the company of others. His lawyer was not allowed to use expert witnesses who could refute the single bomb theory—neither a bomb expert nor a seismologist. ATF informant Carol Howe, who could have testified in support of what the judge

---

[1] Ibid., O'Reilly.

characterized as a conspiracy theory, wasn't allowed to testify. We're reminded of McVeigh's lawyer, Stephen Jones, writing that the State Department diplomatic security service's counterterrorism section distributed photos of the German national Andreas Strassmeir as a suspect in the Oklahoma City bombing with the investigation code number on the leaflet, but the FBI would not seriously consider him a subject of its investigation.[1]

On its face, the single bomb theory seems implausible. How could an ANFO truck bomb do that much damage? The part of the building closest to the truck was reinforced concrete without windows, too strong for an ANFO bomb, according to experts, to do much damage. The building blew from the inside out, projecting pieces into the Athenian restaurant northwest of the Murrah Building. A mile away, window frames had been pushed back two feet. No one has fully explained why witnesses felt electricity running through their bodies before the blast or explained the thunderlike sound and blue light flashes. All this was strange, but what is more strange is that ANFO doesn't cause sparks to blow out of computers before it blasts, nor could it blow out elevator doors on the opposite side of the building. It could have been a backpack nuke or a neutron bomb or a fuel-air explosive or demolition charges or perhaps many explosions at the same time, as Pentagon experts concluded, according to the

---

[1] Stephen Jones, *Others Unknown* (New York, 2001), 334.

March 20, 1996 issue of *Strategic Investment*: "A classified report prepared by two independent Pentagon experts has concluded that the destruction of the Federal building in Oklahoma City last April was caused by five separate bombs."[1] Perhaps most damning of all for the single bomb theory is the report of a ten-second difference between two distinct seismic waves of the same amplitude on April 19, pointing directly at two explosions. Many witnesses said the building blew from the inside out, and explosions, according to witnesses, actually burst through the roof. Yet the whole story is upside down given that even more witnesses heard two explosions. What about the witnesses, not just one, who saw men wiring columns in the basement garage with what looked like C4 explosives?

We could ask the historians of this period, which is still obscured by Clinton who understood everything but couldn't do everything, or even just ask the historians of this particular event who are looking for forgotten motifs and secret circumstances, to include one piece of evidence. According to David Hoffman, author of the increasingly relevant and indicative 1998 Feral House book *The Oklahoma City Bombing and the Politics of Terror*, Tri-State Trucking from Joplin, Missouri delivered six 25- to 35-pound boxes to the Murrah building two weeks before the blast. The boxes were emblazoned HIGH EXPLOSIVE, and looked just like the bomb with a timer set for ten after nine that was

---

[1] Cited in Gore Vidal, *Perpetual War for Perpetual Peace* (New York, 2002), 120.

pulled from the building wreckage. Other bombs were found inside, such as five-gallon containers of exotic mercury fulminate, residues of which were found on the scene. Reporters spoke of bomb teams diffusing numerous bombs, as did others, including Governor Keating, who later said he never mentioned other bombs.[1] Although the official story was that there were no other bombs, the ATF later admitted that there were other devices. GSA workers describe an incredible arsenal, including an antitank missile in the ATF magazine. All of this was stored directly above the America's Kids Day Care Center.

There are more details, such as the unidentified soldier's severed leg or the ATF agents immediately on the scene in full combat gear, or other agents who may or may not have been trapped inside the building during the bombing, such as Luke Franey. This is the IRS criminal investigator whom authorities placed inside at the time of the blast. Another man troubled by the way reality was misaligned with representation, was Sergeant Terrance Yeakey, who appears to have been the most honest man in all of this. Yeakey contradicted the official version of Franey's activity; Yeakey saw Franey run into the building, which was suspiciously empty of ATF agents, some of whom told eyewitnesses, "We were tipped by our pagers not to come into work today."[2] Franey was in full riot gear.

---

[1] Cf., Timeline.

[2] Ian Williams Goddard, *Prevailing Winds*, 9, quotes *20/20* eyewitness testimony, broadcast January 17, 1997.

Was Yeakey's grisly demise, his so-called suicide after dragging his bleeding body to a quiet spot in the country, an assassination fostered by his doubts about what happened on April 19 and what was said about it? Will his suspicious death and the interviews on the January 17, 1997 edition of the ABC magazine *20/20* of numerous witnesses who saw Bomb Squad people on the scene prior to the blasts and fire trucks headed to the scene prior to the blasts will all of this find its way into history? The *20/20* investigation revealed that a tip was made to the Department of Justice twenty-four minutes before the blast and no action was taken. As with the Lusitania, Pearl Harbor, and many of our other examples, Oklahoma City has the hallmark of an indirect defensive attack. We know, thanks to Goddard's *Prevailing Winds* article, that US District Judge Wayne Alley did not go to his offices across from the federal building on April 19 because he was warned against it. The court apparently found out about his statements regarding foreknowledge and he was taken off the Oklahoma City bombing trial case, although the court simply said Alley couldn't be unbiased because his offices were damaged by the blast.

Goddard goes on to describe a fabricated tale of an ATF agent and DEA agent freefalling five floors in the elevator, surviving, and going on to save other survivors. Commercial elevator inspectors say the story was false and that the elevator in question was unscathed. Perhaps the most obvious detail in the charade was McVeigh's double, who didn't even look like him, but said he was Tim McVeigh when going office to office, ostensibly looking for a job in the Murrah building.

Neither the real nor fake McVeigh needed a job because they both worked for what McVeigh told his sister was "a Special Forces Group involved in criminal activity."[1] The public should be more curious about John Doe number two; were he and other operatives double or agents? We should ask if McVeigh were deployed as a useful idiot by them, or by the government, or both. The consequence of this attack was the predictable enactment of anti-terrorism legislation increasing police power that had been resisted for decades by civil rights advocates. The militia movement seemed to retreat, but we suspect that it simply reverted to its roots in the Army, particularly the reserves.[2]

12.

We were amused, but not surprised when French authors Jean-Charles Brisard and Guillaume Dasquié appeared on CNN regarding their book *Bin Laden: The Forbidden Truth*,[3] for a

---

[1] Gore Vidal, *Perpetual War for Perpetual Peace* (New York, 2002), 113.
[2] Tod Ensign, "The Militia Military Connection," *Covert Action Quarterly* Summer 1995, 13-16.
[3] Brisard and Dasquié's *Ben Laden: la vérité interdite*. (Paris, 2001) is not to be confused with the hot-selling *L'Effroyable imposture* by Thierry Meyssan (Paris, 2002), which makes the incorrect claim on its cover that no plane crashed into the Pentagon.

moment, just long enough for one of them to be introduced. The interview was abruptly cancelled without explanation. They suddenly disappeared from the screen before they could say a word about their book. This incident, this bit by which the truth was revealed, indicates how complete truth is forbidden, at least on CNN.

Revelations concerning Osama bin Laden's financial ties to other members of the Saudi ruling class, caused a stir in Switzerland, where an injunction was placed on the book. The authors hope to prove their assertions in court. This could explain why the CNN interview was cancelled. Or perhaps it was Brisard's interview with John O'Neill, the deputy director of the FBI who resigned in August 2001 out of resentment for heavy-handed political pressure linked to oil that prevented him from apprehending al-Qaeda terrorists. If this is the case, it implies a sophisticated cover-up.

Another more likely rationale is that powerful forces object to the well-documented chronicle of discrete Afghan-American negotiations, particularly those under the second Bush's administration. As Marcus Aurelius writes, "What follows is ever closely linked to what precedes; it is not a procession of isolated events, merely obeying the laws of sequence, but a rational continuity."[1]

---

[1] Marcus Aurelius, *Meditations* (New York, 1964), 73.

The Taliban overture to the newly appointed president, made in February 2001 through a London paper, resulted in Berlin meetings. As early as May, however, US diplomats threatened to overthrow the Taliban by military force. Meanwhile, a U.N. representative held talks with the Afghan king about his return, from exile, to power in Kabul. The plan to invade Afghanistan and establish a post-Taliban regime was made long before September 11.

To put this in context, Brisard and Dasquié describe the Clinton administration's failed efforts to deal with the Taliban through the United Nations. Much of the record is still opaque, although the book begins to piece together the mosaic with choice details.

Six months after his August 1998 launch of seventy-five cruise missiles at Khost and Jalalabad, in response to al-Qaeda attacks on US embassies in Africa, Clinton tried to negotiate with Mullah Omar. Clinton seemed to think that Omar—the one-eyed peasant soldier who announced that he welcomed bin Laden in Afghanistan—would extradite the notorious Saudi and close his terrorist training camps. US companies could then build oil pipelines and at long last obtain a return on their investment in drilling rights in Khazakstan and other Central Asian countries.

Although it was a far-fetched plan, Clinton had Pakistani Prime Minister Nawaz Sharif send the head of his intelligence service, the Inter-Services Intelligence Agency (ISI), to Kandahar where he supposedly convinced Omar to cooperate. Sharif then ordered the ISI to close the multinational training camps in the so-called tribal zone along the border with Afghanistan; he was deposed five days later, in October 1999, in a military coup.

It took some time, but the Clinton administration met with Sharif's successor, General Musharaf, along with the Taliban ambassador and information ministers; in Islamabad regarding extradition of Afghanistan's most-wanted guest. This was in January 2000, just as aid money was released to Afghanistan and discrete U.N.-sponsored meetings resumed between the six plus two countries (Pakistan, Iran, China, Uzbekistan, Tajikistan, and Turkmenistan, plus Russia and the United States).

As relations warmed, the Taliban's minister of foreign affairs attended a conference at the Middle East Institute in September 2000 and another member of the delegation met with the administration's counterterrorism coordinator, Michael Sheehan. The State Department publicly acknowledged the work of the six plus two group in a Moscow press conference and it seemed as though the group would facilitate peace negotiations between the Taliban and the Northern Alliance.

Then something changed, although it is not clear why relations soured. After the 2000 presidential vote was settled, the six-plus-two talks stopped, and Michael Sheehan denounced the Taliban in Congress as a supporter of terrorism. As he prepared to leave office, in December 2000, one of Clinton's final diplomatic acts was to persuade the U.N. Security Council to strengthen the moderate economic sanctions imposed against the Taliban in 1999.

Had new facts surfaced? Those of us with conspiracy-minded suspicions might wonder whether someone, say, from a corporation that has aspired to build a pipeline through Afghanistan for many years, encouraged the Taliban to dig in their heels and wait for a better deal from Bush. Speculation is tempting, but the facts, as revealed through the Brisard and Dasquié book which we have checked and supplemented, are incriminating enough.

13.

The Taliban announced their overture to Bush on the front page of *The Times* of London on February 5, 2001: "Taleban offers US deal to deport bin Laden." The short article quoted the Afghan foreign minister as saying "We hope the new American Administration will be more flexible and engage with us." The United States responded a week later via its U.N. mission, requesting what it called a "continuing dialogue" with the Taliban.

The ensuing Berlin talks hosted by the U.N. secretary general's personal representative, Fransesc Vendrell, are described by the authors of *Bin Laden: The Forbidden Truth* through two primary sources: a report by the Secretary General of the Security Council entitled "The Situation in Afghanistan and its Implications for International Peace and Security" and by Naiz Naik, former Pakistani minister of foreign affairs. The goals of the negotiation were to convince the Taliban to "sign an armistice with the Northern Alliance, compose a national unity government, and extradite Osama bin Laden."

The Afghan minister of foreign affairs refused to take part in May 15th discussions with the Northern Alliance because they were hosted by the same United Nations that voted for sanctions against the Taliban. According to Naik, the US delegation reportedly evoked "a 'military option' against the Taliban," although one of its members, Tom Simmons, former US ambassador to Islamabad under Clinton, denies this threat was clearly stated.

The authors cite many reasons to doubt this partial denial.

First, Vendrell held contemporaneous talks with exiled Afghan king in Rome and discussed convening what the U.N. called "an extraordinary *loya jirga*," or grand council.

Second, the US State Department released a poll taken of 5,000 Afghans finding that fifty percent agreed that the former king could best address current problems.

Third, the authors point to a June 1 meeting, what the U.N. called a "brainstorming session," in Washington between Vendrell, National Security Advisor Condoleeza Rice, Assistant Secretary of State for South Asia Christina Rocca, and British observers. Rocca attained her experience overthrowing Afghan governments when she was the CIA officer handling mujahedeen resistance fighters. The newly appointed State Department official would go to Pakistan in August to speak about oil and demand the extradition of bin Laden.

Fourth, a communiqué by the spokesperson for the French minister of foreign affairs regarding his meeting with Vendrell supported international efforts to have the king meet with representatives of Afghan society. Vendrell also discussed what the U.N. called "the need for a comprehensive approach to the Afghanistan conflict" with Joschka Fischer, Germany's foreign minister.

Fifth, messages were sent by what the book vaguely names as "l'Occident" to the Taliban, stating, as the authors phrase it, that "an option against them is being studied to capture Osama bin Laden," and "discussions have been undertaken with the former king to retake power in Kabul." Did Christina Rocca make these threats when she demanded the extradition of bin Laden on August 2 of the Taliban ambassador in Islamabad? Were these threats relayed to the Taliban by others, for example the Pakistani Inter-Services Intelligence, as the *Guardian* and other papers reported?

The authors choose to stop their narrative without commenting on the implications. If these threats were made, they cast new light on the FBI-confirmed wire transfer of $100,000 from Lt. General Mahmood Ahmad, the Inter-Services

Intelligence's top man who was having breakfast with congressmen in Washington on the morning of the attacks, to Mohammed Atta, alleged head terrorist in the operation, in the summer of 2001. The money either financed a preemptive offensive on September 11, or an indirect defensive attack.

Is it possible that Bush strategists naively announced they would wage war with the Taliban in Afghanistan, rather than launch a surprise attack as Clinton did, because they thought Mullah Omar would respond agreeably to these threats? Or were the threats designed to provoke a preemptive strike that the US defense establishment would allow to happen or even an operation carried out by infiltrators that in either case, would serve as a pretext to invade Afghanistan? Did the United States indirectly stage a defensive attack against itself using people such as General Ahmad or Mohammed Atta?

14.

CIA Director George Tenet warned Congress, according to a representative quoted on National Public Radio the day of the hijackings, about a so-called asymmetrical threat the week before 9-11. Did Tenet, who made a trip of his own to Islamabad in May, know about the $100,000 transfer? Did Tenet meet or speak with General Mahmood Ahmad, who was in Washington on

September 11? Was Tenet unaware of the general's support for al-Qaeda or not? Either way Tenet's response, whatever he says, is untenable. Although this fact is now disputed, the CIA knew, or at least thought, that Atta met, in 2001, with Iraqi intelligence in Prague and that Iraqis were sending money to al-Qaeda in Pakistan. How was a man like Atta allowed to enter the country, muchless receive advanced military training from the US Air Force, as reported in *Newsweek* on September 15.[1]

We may never get to the bottom of the cesspit formed around September 11, but if threats were made, the response seems predictable, especially given how Taliban warriors doubted Washington's resolve. What is irrational, except from a narrow class perspective, is complicity in creating the pretext for a war to pump feed the arms and oil industries. Contrary to economic theories of imperialism, typically applied to the nineteenth century European experience, history shows that the costs for infrastructure and security to colonize a country can exceed the riches gained by the empire in raw materials.[2] For example, costs associated with the September 11 attacks and the US response should be added to the defense budget because they were at many levels the consequences of US troops being stationed in Saudi Arabia and US military support for Israel. While the masses

---

[1] George Wehrfritz, et.al., "Alleged Hijackers May Have Trained at U.S. Bases," *Newsweek*, September 15, 2001.

[2] Alan Hodgart, *Economics of European Imperialism,* (New York, 1977). Nationalism, power politics, military expediency—these explain more about imperialism than access to raw materials, new markets, and an outlet for surplus capital, according to Rondo Cameron in *A Concise Economic History of the World,* (Oxford, 1989), 321–2.

pay back war debts, the elite almost always profit from the extraordinary military consumption that feeds our rulers' greed and lust for dominion.

15.

Textbooks on US diplomacy depict US-Saudi relations as being warmer than the kingdom's ties with Britain and France because of America's guarded sympathy for Arab self-determination after the First World War. The US legation in Riyadh opened in 1942 and in 1943 President Franklin Roosevelt declared the defense of Saudi Arabia in the vital interest of the United States and granted it Lend-Lease Act assistance through Britain. In 1944, Saudi Arabia opened a legation in Washington.

Although FDR was both pro-Arab and pro-Zionist, he, unlike his successors, appreciated the Saudi declaration of war on Germany in early 1945. President Roosevelt and Saudi King Abd al-Aziz ibn Saoud met on February 14, 1945 aboard the cruiser *Quincy* in the Suez Canal, after the king's two-day cruise from Jeddah aboard a US destroyer. The two leaders primarily discussed the migration of European Jews to Palestine at the end of the Second World War.

The king was implacably against it and instead in favor of a European homeland, basing his argument on the assertion that

Arabs hadn't done anything to the European Jews. He also insisted on independence for Syria and Lebanon. We read several accounts of this meeting, but none confirm contention in *Forbidden Truth* that a deal was struck on oil, namely US military support for the Saudi regime against its internal enemies in exchange for unlimited access to oil. Perhaps something has been airbrushed out of American accounts and their French sources will enlighten us.

What happened at Bitter Lake, as far as we can tell, was that FDR promised to keep the king informed about all US plans for the region and not make any changes without consultations; subsequent letters suggest he was sincere. FDR died shortly after the trip and Truman betrayed the promise by the way he supported the Zionist cause. An important US-Saudi pipeline project nonetheless began after the war and was finished in 1950.

The American Empire is currently ruled by the likes of Richard Cheney, a man who has clear allegiances to the defense and petroleum industries as former secretary of defense and CEO of Halliburton—a company feeding on defense and oil drilling contracts that is now under investigation for including its future overruns in current revenues and other dubious accounting practices. He seems too savvy to have made a video for his accounting firm, praising its practices. The president himself is depicted in the superb biography *Fortunate Son* by J.H. Hatfield as following in his father's oil-prospecting footsteps by trading on his name in Texas and Bahrain. Oil and stock options are in the blood of this boy from Midland Texas, but when George W. Bush formed his own drilling company, James R. Bath invested money in the project, possibly from clients like Sheikh Khalid bin Mahfouz, once King Fahed's banker and Osama's brother in law. It could easily have been money from Osama's brother Sheikh Salem bin Laden, another Bath client, who gave Bush his start as a prospector. When the BCCI scandal erupted, Bush tried to deny that he had ever conducted business with Bath, but tax records proved otherwise. Bush then denied knowing the money came from Saudis such as Mahfouz, whose charity organizations have for years provided essential financial support to al-Qaeda, according to both *Fortunate Son* and *Forbidden Truth*.

Mahfouz's company Nimir Petroleum invested heavily in Kazakhstan exploration rights. Along with Delta Oil Company, Mahfouz tried to work out a deal for the construction of an oil pipeline from the Daulatabad gas fields in Turkmenistan, through Afghanistan, to Multan in Pakistan. Delta's partner in this five-billion-dollar joint venture was the American corporation Unocal, which took its case to Congress on the need for a stable government in Afghanistan so it could build the pipeline. Mahfouz, according to Brisard and Dasquié, was supposed to get the Taliban to come around. Apparently, he wasn't up to the job and the Pentagon relieved him and a prime minister more favorable to a pipeline deal was installed.

We were not surprised to learn how extensive Osma bin Laden's support network for terrorism has become, or even that his family remained in close touch throughout his exile. Some family members most likely support his *fatwa* against the United Sates. As for Bush family ties to the bin Laden family, Brisard's account weaves tight nets around the Carlyle Group and BCCI, what the Justice Department called "the Bank of Crooks and Criminals."

The bin Ladens sold their stake in Carlyle on October 26, but this cannot hide the *Wall Street Journal* report that former President George H.W. Bush traveled to Saudi Arabia in 1998 and 2000 on behalf of the Carlyle Group and met with the bin Laden family. George W. Bush himself happened to have worked for a subsidiary of a Carlyle Corporation, which, as a giant defense contractor, profits handsomely from war.

The group, coincidentally, was meeting on September 11 at the luxurious Ritz Hotel in Washington's West End. We have settled back in the plush seats and taken in the surroundings. We've even tried to imagine, over the piano player, what it would be like to be callous, ruthless businessmen. We find that all the fancy molding is misaligned, as if the contract had gone to the lowest bidder and, as is so often the case in business, no one really cared about the outcome.

16.

Few things rouse our suspicions more about 9-11 than the way members of the bin Laden family residing in the United States were shuttled out of the country on a private jet right after the attacks—when no other planes, other than military, were allowed to fly. Was the FBI consulted on this move? Was George Bush the Elder at the White House on September 11 and what about allegations, stated on *BBC Newsnight*, that FBI agents were told, after the Bush election scam,[1] to "back off" the bin Laden family?

In an incredible November 6, 2001 roundtable discussion hosted by Greg Palast, author Joe Trento—*Secret History of the CIA*—revealed an incriminating FBI document (Case ID—199-Eye WF 213 589). The case involves thwarted FBI efforts to investigate the World Assembly of Muslim Youth run by Abdullah bin Laden in Falls Church, Virginia. Another bin Laden brother, Omar, and four of the hijackers lived in nearby residences. Trento says "The FBI wanted to investigate these guys. This is not something that they didn't want to do—they wanted to, they weren't permitted to."

---

[1] Greg Palast makes the case for the rigged 2000 election in Florida in *The Best Democracy Money Can Buy* (London, 2002), 6-43; the Collier brothers show fraudulent elections have taken place for years: James and Kenneth Collier, *Votescam*, (New York, 1992).

Greg Palast was on the case with follow up: "The US Treasury has not frozen WAMY's assets, and when we talked to them, they insisted they were a charity. Yet, just weeks ago, Pakistan expelled WAMY operatives. And India claimed that WAMY was funding an organization linked to bombings in Kashmir. And the Philippine military has accused WAMY of funding Muslim insurgency. The FBI did look into WAMY, but, for some reason, agents were pulled off the trail."

An even more shocking revelation on the show, by former State Department employee Michael Springmann, is that the CIA has been working closely with bin Laden and his operatives in Jeddah since 1987. Springmann was "repeatedly ordered by high level State Department officials to issue visas to unqualified applicants." His complaints went unanswered and he now asserts the operation was "an effort to bring recruits, rounded up by Osama bin Laden, to the US for terrorist training by the CIA." At the UnansweredQuestions press conference Springmann made the point, that based on the public record, fifteen of the nineteen skyjackers received their visas from the same consulate.[1] In July 2002, Secretary of State Colin Powell asked for the resignation of the department's highest-ranking consular official, Mary Ryan, because of a visa bribery scandal in Qatar and an express visa program involving travel agents in Saudi Arabia. No mention was

---

[1] UnansweredQuestions.org, "9-11 and the Public Safety: Seeking Answers and Accountability," 30.

made in press reports of allegations by Springmann about CIA intervention in Jeddah.[1]

We need to know about the skyjackers and the training they received in the United States. How is it that three of them listed Pensacola Naval Air Station on their drivers' licenses and car registrations? This would be Saeed Alghamdi, Ahmad Alnami, and Ahmed Alghamdi, according to an article in *Newsweek*.[2] Who financed their training? Was it Saudi Arabia or the United States? How did people funded and trained by the state, supposedly in the service of one state or another, wind up committing terrorist acts? Was it just a big screw up or was it by design of the US government or had the terrorists infiltrated the US military to further their aims?

This screwup excuse, which reminds us of Hannibal Lechter's contempt for FBI ineptitude in *Silence of the Lambs*, is probably more fiction than fact. Aukai Collins, author of *My Jihad*, is more believable than the bureau's denial when he says that he spied on skyjacker Hani Hanjour in Phoenix. The bureau does admit that Collins spied on Islamic and Arab communities in Phoenix, but denies Collins provided information on Hanjour. Collins insists the bureau "knew everything about the guy."[3]

---

[1] Susan Schmidt and Glenn Kessler, "Powell Seeks Top Consular Official's Resignation," *Washington Post*, July 11, 2002, 13.

[2] George Wehrfritz, et al. "Alleged Hijackers May Have Trained at U.S. Bases," *Newsweek*, September 15, 2001. Note that these names could also be spelled Al Ghamdi, Al Nami, and Al Ghamdi.

[3] John McWethy, "FBI Was Warned of Sept. 11 Hijacker," *ABCNews.com*, May 23, 2002.

Hani, as Collins calls him, was living with others in an apartment together, drank alcohol, and "messed around with girls and stuff like that."

Hanjour first came to Arizona in 1990, and by then Tucson was already "a well-established stop for Islamic militants."[1] Alkhifa, a fundraising group for the jihad in Afghanistan, established an office in Tucson in the eighties. When the Soviet Union retreated from Afghanistan, Alkhifa merged with al-Qaeda. The FBI used infiltrators to monitor, for example, an associate of Sheikh Omar Abdul Rahman giving instruction in explosives. From 1996 to 2001 Hanjour attended various flight schools and studied English in Arizona. Hanjour has been described by his instructors as a poor, timid student who nonetheless obtained his commercial license with a multiengine rating in 1999. He would train on a commercial airliner simulator in Phoenix in February 2001, but by August 2001 he was attempting to use planes at Bowie Maryland's Freeway Airport where instructors felt he was "unable to fly solo," which makes us suspicious of the assertion by authorities that Hanjour was the pilot aboard American Airlines flight 77 that crashed into the Pentagon.[2]

In fact, we are suspicious about anything the FBI says about the skyjackers given their massive reversal in less than a

---

[1] Jim Yardley and Jo Thomas, "For Agent in Phoenix, the Cause of Many Frustrations Extended to His Own Office," *New York Times*, June 19, 2001.
[2] *Prince George's Journal*, September 18, 2001.

year—from making discoveries of letters in the luggage of the suspects that proved their intentions to complete absence of a "paper trail." Could it be that there is a paper trail that has been burned by the agency? In an April 19 speech to the Commonwealth Club in San Francisco, FBI Director Mueller said: "…we have not uncovered a single piece of paper—either here in the United States or in the treasure trove of information that turned up in Afghanistan and elsewhere—that mentioned any aspect of the Sept. 11 plot."[1] Moreover, we have not forgotten the fact that six of the nineteen skyjackers on the FBI's second list, released on September 27, 2001, turned out to be alive. What's more, Hani Hanjour was not listed as the pilot of American Airlines flight 77 on the second list.[2] Tucson resident Dick Fojut has stayed on the case: Following his e-mail letter to Arizona Republican Senator John Kyl, Fojut lists URLS to numerous papers in Britain and elsewhere, including a CNN.com correction, indicating that the identities of they skyjackers are still obscure and that possibly *seven* listed by the FBI are still alive.

We share Fojut's suspicions about Mohammed Atta's luggage containing an admission of the attacks and not making it aboard the suicide flight. We had almost forgotten how fantastically Atta's passport supposedly flew out of his pocket as

---

[1] Michael Collins Piper "FBI Admits No Evidence Links 'Hijackers' to 911," American Free Press, May 18, 2002, also Katty Kay, "FBI fails to find terror trail," BBC News, May 1, 2002.
[2] Syed Adeeb, "Six Men Identified by FBI as Dead Hijackers are Alive," *Truedemocracy.net*, September 27, 2001.

the plane crashed into the World Trade Center and landed on the street nearby. With these suspicious details in mind, what do we make of the fact that the CIA monitored ringleader Mohammed Atta in Frankfurt from January to May 2000; Atta then entered the United States in June to pursue his dreams of becoming a suicide pilot. Who followed up on this and his subsequent trip? Someone certainly noticed when he brazenly picked fights in restaurants and bars up and down the East Coast?[1] Why is there such a discrepancy between eyewitnesses placing Atta in Venice Beach, Florida, a CIA training place, just prior to the attacks and the FBI account?

The authorities know much more than they are letting on about this operation and we raise our eyebrows at the return of Iran-Contra figures such as Elliott Abrams, who pleaded guilty to withholding information from Congress, but was pardoned by Bush the Elder; at the return of Otto Reich, a State Department covert operations boss against the Sandinistas who received the leader of the Venezuelan coup in 2002 at the White House and reportedly discussed the plan at length; Richard Armitage, the current deputy secretary of state, who probably knows everything about the operation because of his Pakistani intelligence contacts; John Negroponte, the United Nations ambassador and former ambassador to Honduras when the Contras used the country as a base; and John Poindexter, who was convicted of conspiracy,

---

[1] Dennis Hopsicker, *Mohammed Atta's Venice Flying Circus* (video), From the Wilderness 2002.

making false statements to Congress, and obstructing congressional inquiries. He now heads a new Pentagon counterterrorism office.

17.

The FBI is finally being criticized from within. Some toe the party line, such as the Phoenix agent who claims his now scandalous memo recommending a nationwide flight school dragnet for Islamic terrorists would not have impeded the 9-11 attacks. Others, such as Minneapolis FBI Inspector General Coleen Rowley, have been more candid about what was done at headquarters to impede investigations and what could have been done. Her most serious allegations, beyond David Frasca altering of her FISA search warrant applications, remain secret. We do know that she and her colleagues joked about bin Laden having accomplices in headquarters, we also know how humor reveals truths by dispelling anger. As the attacks were unfolding, Frasca actually called Rowley and told her not to investigate Moussaoui because Minneapolis might "screw up" something going on elsewhere in the country—what might that have been?[1]

---

[1] A story in Britain's *Eye Spy* (issue eight, 2002), appearing without attribution, states that Barbara Olson, wife of the solicitor general, was a "deep agent." She died on American Airlines flight 77 while allegedly, "supervising apparently a

Rowley has since testified before the Senate that she has received hundreds of e-mail messages voicing similar complaints about the denizens of the J. Edgar Hoover Building on Pennsylvania Avenue, between Capitol Hill and the White House, who fill roles in a vast, self-protecting hierarchy.

David Shippers, the attorney who masterminded the low-blow impeachment of Clinton, nonetheless raises our suspicions with the allegations of his client, Chicago FBI Special Agent Robert Wright. To guard the cover on an intelligence investigation, we hear on National Public Radio that Wright's well-developed criminal investigation into one of bin Laden's major financiers was shut down. The financier went on to send wads of money to al-Qaeda. What do Shipper's old buddies in the House think of that? Will they back the man who backed them or will they back the state?

Another deputy director of the embattled FBI has resigned after the attacks. Thomas Pickard determined the September 11 attacks were carried out by a self-contained cell out of Germany, then lost the "fire in the belly," as he told the *Washington Post*. Why? Was Pickard aware how closely CIA was monitoring this Hamburg cell?

Is there any truth to the report from reliable sources in *Le Figaro* that a CIA officer met with bin Laden in his Dubai hospital suite, as late as July 2001? Did he communicate precise

_____

dozen or so agents to see that the terrorist cells were safely escorted across the country for a big sting."

information about attacks inside the United States? The CIA denies the meeting took place, but its denials aren't always true. Was there a predictable turf war between the CIA and FBI,[1] or worse, conflicting goals, for and against, terror?

18.

Forbidden Truth, which deserves to be translated and published in English but seems to be taboo for the US publishing industry, opens in the Plaza Hotel in Manhattan at the end of July 2001 with Brisard interviewing John O'Neill, former antiterrorist coordinator for the FBI and then deputy director of the New York office in charge of national security. O'Neill spoke about his investigations into al-Qaeda attacks on the *USS Cole* in the Persian Gulf and U.S. military installations in Saudi Arabia, concluding that American oil interests prevented the State Department from applying pressure to King Fahed. "All the responses, all the keys to dismantling the Osama bin Laden organization," O'Neill said, "are found in Saudi Arabia."

Rupert Cornwell of the *Independent* describes O'Neill as, "a flamboyant, driven man fond of sharp suits and attractive women," had, "been involved in all of America's biggest recent

---

[1] Colorful historical examples of which are documented in Mark Reibling's *Wedge* (New York, 1994).

terrorist cases: from Islamic extremists' initial attack on the Centre in 1993 to the 1995 Oklahoma City bombing; from the long and inconclusive probe into the mystery of TWA Flight 800 to the attacks on US bases in Saudi Arabia in 1995 and 1996, the US embassy bombings in Africa in 1998, and last year's attack on the destroyer *USS Cole* in the port of Aden, Yemen." Cornwell goes on to say that, with the exception of Flight 800 and Oklahoma City, "O'Neill established links between every incident and Mr. bin Laden's group."[1]

Brisard recalls that O'Neill was only half-surprised when he read the report on the economic environment of bin Laden that traced direct economic links between him and the kingdom in July 2001, contradicting what was said in public by both parties. O'Neill thought that state interests were given higher priority than the fight against terrorism and resigned with deep resentments in August 2001. He became director of security for the World Trade Center, where, according to researcher Sherman Skolnick, O'Neill was working on the suicide skyjacker threat, and where he perished on September 11.

What's more astonishing in this spy-work-gone-awry scenario is that the first arrest warrant by Interpol to catch Osama bin Laden, according to *Forbidden Truth*, was made at the request of the Libyan interior minister. Osama lived in Jabala-Larde while supporting the Libyan Islamic Fighting Group (Jama

---

[1] Rupert Cornwell, "The FBI's sharp-dressed, sharp-tongued expert on Al Qa'ida, who died in Twin Towers," *The Independent*, June 18, 2002.

al-Islamiya al-Muqatila). The British MI5 prepared an operation with this group to kill Kadhafi in 1996, but never pulled it off.

The Libyan dictator is inscrutable—why, unless it was under favorable terms from the United States, did he agree to have defense lawyers for Lockerbie terror suspect Adbelbaset Ali Mohmed al-Megrahi's[1] fall, so to speak, on exploding baggage. They were offered exculpatory evidence from disillusioned CIA anti-terror agent Robert Baer, but they reportedly refused to see it. Baer's documents and records point to Iran paying $11 million to the Popular Front for the Liberation of Palestine-General Command. After September 11, which Kadhafi denounced, and the advent of the war on terrorism, Libyan intelligence gladly gave MI6 the names of al-Muqatila members living in London, as if they didn't already know. Al-Megrahi's appeal is now underway. We are curious to see whether justice is carried out or is the victim of a deal, perhaps offered by Assistant US Secretary of State for the Middle East William Burns to Libyan intelligence officer Musa Kusa when they met in England in January 2002. Was a deal struck whereby Libya agrees to accept blame for Lockerbie and pay compensation to the victims' families in exchange for removal from the State Department's state-terror list and the US oil deals that would flow from this change in status?

---

[1] Alternately, Adb el Baset Ali Mohamed al-Megrahi

We agree with Bush when he denounces state-sponsored terror but we go further ahead and test the state-massacre thesis on the United States and Britain. We recall, for example, the CIA's psychological warfare operation in Chile: As the Pinochet coup transpired, the left was blamed for highly publicized atrocities perpetrated by right-wing operatives, atrocities that escalated day by day, increasing social tension, atrocities that eventually included mass beheadings.[1] But the most poignant example is the 1993 bombing of the World Trade Center. Lest we forget the facts that emerged from the case, let it be remembered here and everywhere that the FBI infiltrator showed the terrorists how to make the bomb and where to put it; he was pulled off the case and Ramsey Yousef took his place.

19.

Ascribing motivation is always dangerous, but facts and protagonists tend to speak for themselves in laying bare the ruling passions afflicting the ruling class. Major US oil companies have invested billions in Kazakhstan's Tengiz oil field, often in dubious ways that have profited its dictatorship, as Seymour Hersh demonstrates in his *New Yorker* article "The Price of Oil."

---

[1] Donald Freed and Fred Landis, *Death in Washington* (Westport, 1980), 108-13.

ExxonMobil and BP Amoco are under grand jury investigation for bribing foreign officials, and researcher Michael Ruppert notes that these bribes were made when Cheney, then with Halliburton, was a member of the nation's oil advisory board.

Another illustrative aspect of the investigation is an illegal, due to sanctions against Tehran, swap effected by Mobil between Kazakhstan and Iran. The swap was a way around transport problems—Kazakh oil went to Iran across the Caspian Sea in exchange for Iranian oil sold on the world market and shipped from the Persian Gulf—that never really panned out. Although only one swap was made and Mobil didn't profit from the deal, it appears to have been highly involved in the swap, which demonstrates the lengths to which US companies will go to move Kazakh oil.

The stalled westward-oriented pipeline, an American project, is planned to take Caspian oil to Ceyhan, Turkey, and on to the Mediterranean. US companies, meanwhile, refuse to pay high rates for using the Russian line that opened in summer 2001. Those zeros in return columns on investment reports don't go over well in boardrooms. A trans-Afghan pipeline, although seemingly impossible to defend regardless of who holds power in Kabul, has been the solution promoted for years by western oil companies. Afghan Prime Minister Hamid Karzai adamantly supports the project.

Thousands of US troops have moved into Uzbekistan, Tajikistan, and Kyrgyzstan. The defense and oil people around

Bush lust for oil and obviously don't mind war to get it, no matter how costly. How much would people like Tenet and Cheney pay with their souls if in fact they knew about the September 11 attacks in advance and then did nothing to stop them, if they committed contributory negligence in something of an inside job?

20.

The public knows that US statesmen planned to overthrow the Taliban by military force. The public has heard evidence that the FBI knew al-Qaeda intended to fly planes into the World Trade Center and Pentagon. The public may even have read in a national weekly about suspicions that the US Navy taught some of the skyjackers how to fly because they were living on base in Pensacola. The public, to a more limited extent, may have read in dailies about specific advanced warning given to and by the US government and other people in positions of authority. We would like to present evidence of a more seemingly miscellaneous, but possibly even more indicative nature.

What, for example, were the results of the investigation into unusually high put options, essentially on bets that a stock will fall, on American Airlines and United Airlines stock the week prior to the attack? Is the case being examined in a fair way? Or, as Michael Ruppert of *From the Wilderness* implies in his excellent

"Timeline Surrounding September 11," was a high-ranking CIA official, Buzzy Krongard, allowed to show the cards to his banking colleagues in advance—the same firm that made so many put options on United Airlines was managed by Krongard until 1998. Why did another banker, Mayo Shattuck III, resign from the top post of this A.B. or Alex Brown unit of Deutsche Bank on September 15?[1] Some experts estimate that $22 million in profits were obtained as a result of the United and American put options—others have much higher estimates, such as the former German Minister of Technology Andreas von Bülow, who puts the figure at $15 billion.[2]

Von Bülow, a sixty-four-year-old former state secretary in the Defense Ministry and federal investigator who has written a book about the CIA, said the assailants left "tracks behind them like a herd of stampeding elephants" and that "clues were left behind like a child's game of hide-and-seek, which were to be followed." He, and many others, want to know, above all, why jets were not scrambled to intercept American Airlines flight 77 when it was heading for Washington? Why was it allowed to come close to the White House and Capitol before heading down the Potomac and circling back, in a coordinated turn simultaneously using the rudder and aileron, to crash full speed

---

[1] The best reporting on this still obscure case is by *From the Wilderness* collaborator Tom Flocco in his three-part series "Profits of Death." See copvcia.com.

[2] Dave Eberhart, "Still Silence From 9-11 Stock Speculation Probe," *NewsMax,* June 3, 2002; Stephen Lebert and Norbert Thomma, "Da sind Spuren wie von einer trampelnden Elefantenherde," *Tagesspiegel,* January 13, 2002.

into a virtually empty side of the Pentagon? Why wasn't the plane shot down by missiles from these buildings? Why did Rumsfeld stay in his office and not go immediately to the National Military Command Center? Was he looking for an alibi when all of this was allowed to happen? Why, when jets were scrambled, were they from a distant base and not from Andrews Air Force Base near Washington, which is charged with protecting the skies over the capital? This lapse is especially glaring given the many warnings for an airline oriented attack.

In his Senate confirmation hearing to become the head of the Joint Chiefs of Staff, General Myers, who was acting chief on Black Tuesday, didn't have adequate answers to these questions. He said he saw the first plane hit and then went into Senator Max Cleland's office for an hour—when he came out NORAD was on the phone and told him the Pentagon had been attacked. As for how and why defense measures were too little too late, Myers mostly said he didn't know and he was confirmed anyway.

Were the anthrax-laced letters, as many investigators believe, an inside job? If so, it will go down in history as one of the classic cases of defensive terror by the state so a few letters terrorized so many people. We explore allegations from reputable scientists in our anthrax chapter (II) that the FBI knows who sent these poison letters, but the man responsible knows too much to be arrested (the authorities are afraid he will talk). Naturally, suspicions are raised when, in the face of so many obvious contradictions, Bush told Congress to limit its investigation into

September 11, 2001. Those of us threatened by anthrax want a thorough investigation; we want Joe Friday, or someone like him, on the case.[1]

21.

In the absence of a Hollywood detective, let's briefly consider the claim that no one knew about the airplanes as weapons scenario. It was of course attempted in 1994; Algerian hijackers planned to ram the Eiffel Tower, but were overtaken when refueling in Marseilles. How can anyone plead ignorance? Director of the House Task Force on Terrorism and Unconventional Warfare Yossef Bodansky wrote about targeting US buildings with hijacked airplanes in his study *Target America: Terrorism in the US Today* in the early nineties. Moreover, Iran has trained suicide pilots since the early eighties, as the CIA well knew, at a modern airport used exclusively for terrorist training exercises.

In 1995, Philippine authorities exposed Project Bojinka, the charred plans found in Ramzi Yousef's burning bomb factory to skyjack planes and ram them into US targets, including the

---

[1] Mike Ruppert, a former Los Angeles cop who skirmishes with the CIA (denoted in his website copvcia.com), could probably do a better, and certainly a more honest job, than the FBI.

Pentagon and World Trade Center. Now that the Pentagon has moved troops into Zamboanga in this "new phase in the war on terrorism," we should keep in mind that the Philippine army colluded with Abu Sayaef for many years, selling the terrorists weapons, letting them hold hostages near military bases, and in a famous incident, allowing them to escape out the back of a church that was supposedly surrounded by government troops.

The clues become even more glaringly clear than in these early, airtight examples. Airman Flight School in Oklahoma told the FBI, in one of two terrorist-related interviews held over the years, that Algerian Zacorias Moussaoui wanted to learn to fly a Boeing 747 and would pay in cash to learn. This is the infamous twentieth man, who would've been the fifth man on Flight 93 that went down in southwest Pennsylvania. He also trained at Pan Am International Flight Academy in Eagen, Minnesota. His instructor explicitly warned a congressman and the FBI that a 747 could be used as a bomb. Moussaoui reportedly only wanted to know how to steer the plane, not take off or land, and inquired about New York airspace. When he was arrested on a passport charge, he was carrying Boeing aircraft and flight manuals, but the Minnesota FBI couldn't look in his computer without a warrant from Washington.

Despite the fact that French intelligence warned American officials prior to the attacks, on September 5 and 6,[1] that

---

[1] James Ridgeway, "U.S. Ignored Warnings From French," *Village Voice*,

Moussaoui was associated with bin Laden, the Justice Department refused, as is rarely the case, to allow the search of the suspect under the Foreign Intelligence Surveillance Act. These surveillance clearance requests under FISA are almost never refused by the Foreign Intelligence Surveillance Court according to a report issued by the Administrative office of the United States Courts. In 2001, all 1,491 wiretap applications by federal agencies were granted. Only three wiretaps have been denied since 1991; a total of 12,658 were granted.[1] Were the three refusals the blatantly flawed applications submitted by Michael Resnick, the Hamas expert, from whom the judges will no longer accept applications?[2] Hadn't this problem been fixed by Freeh's so-called Woods reform whereby the agent in the field certifies the accuracy of the application? Why was Moussaoui protected from being searched? His hard drive later revealed information on aviation-related subjects, including crop-dusting planes, which were subsequently downed across the country. The French also assert that the British refused to put Moussaoui under surveillance when he lived in London.

Yet again, and as late as the G8 summit in Genoa, July 2001, Italian intelligence discovered a plot aimed at assassinating Bush and others by crashing a skyjacked commercial jet into Air

---

May 28, 2002 (quotes *Le Monde*).

[1] Susan Stellin, "Who's Watching? No, Who's Listening In?" *New York Times*, June 3, 2002.

[2] David Johnston, "FBI Inaction Blurred Picture Before Sept. 11," *New York Times*, May 27, 2002.

Force One or a summit building. We scoff at the assertion that using an airliner as weapon was unimaginable because of the response. Airspace over the city of Genoa was restricted to military flights during the G8 summit.

The clearest warning issued by the government came from the State Department on September 7; they wanted the general public to know that groups affiliated with al-Qaeda could be targeting US citizens worldwide. A more precise warning was given to San Francisco Mayor Willie Brown—after receiving a call from undisclosed sources late in evening of September 10, he changed his flight plans. The British government admits, in its indictment of bin Laden, that it knew his associates were warned to return to Afghanistan by September 10 and named September 11 as the action day. Moreover, an Iranian detained in Hanover, Germany warned US officials that an attack would take place the week of September 10.

How much more precise, in terms of foreknowledge, can you get? Try this. *The Washington Times* reports that CIA, on September 10, intercepted calls between al-Qaeda supporters discussing a big attack. *NBC News* reports that a foreign intelligence service heard bin Laden, on September 9, tell his stepmother "In two days you're going to hear big news and you're not going hear from me for a while." Speaking of relatives in the know, Florida Governor Jeb Bush, on September 7, signed an executive order activating the National Guard to protect the state against terrorism.[1]

22.

Another side of this comes from a surprising source, but it supports the thesis that states had foreknowledge or assisted the terrorists who killed nearly three thousand people in New York and Arlington, Virginia. The CIA relies on Israel for Middle East intelligence and warnings of an impending terrorist operation against the United States were made to the FBI and CIA. Two senior Mossad agents gave this notice on a special mission to Washington in July.

Many questions, however, remain regarding the role of our close ally in the whole affair. In his timeline, Michael Ruppert cites CNN for stating that employees of the New York offices of an Israel-based computer company received messages warning about the attacks two hours before they took place. Is this really true?

We remember hearing about an intriguing report by officers at the US Army's School for Advanced Military Studies, discussed

[1] On September 6, 2001 former Senator Gary Hart, co-chairman of the U.S. Commission on National Security for the Twenty First Century, warned Condoleezza Rice, "You must move more quickly on homeland security. An attack is going to happen." Carl Limbacher, *NewsMax.com*, May 29, 2002.

on the front-page of the *Washington Times* on September 10, 2001, the day before the attack. The report characterized the Mossad as a wildcard and said that Israel was capable of targeting the United States as it did in 1967 when it attacked the US communications ship *Liberty* in the Mediterranean to mask the El Arish massacre.[1] Senators investigating the case might want to know what Israeli spymaster Michael Harari thinks about this and about Carl Cameron's FOX News reports regarding large numbers of Israeli spies in connection with the September 11 investigation? The Justice Department denies the story and questioned accounts of the DEA memo exposing the long-running art student spy ring. The memo has now surfaced on the Internet and appears credible in connection with Cameron's FBI sources.

According to the *Washington Post*, reliable sources say that the author of the memo disagreed with the FBI and CIA contention that no spying was taking place.

Jane's Information Group finds it strange that the US media is ignoring the explosive story regarding somewhere from sixty to four hundred Israeli spies who attempted to infiltrate the departments of Justice and Defense over a long period. They were possibly tracking al-Qaeda prior to September 11, which might explain the presence of at least one Israeli counter-terror agent aboard American Airlines flight 11.[2] The Israeli network

---

[1] Israeli massacre of Egyptian prisoners in El Arish in the Sinai Desert.
[2] Intelligence Online, *Insight* Magazine, Salon and Fox have reported on the case, but we learned a great deal from John Sugg, "Update: The Spies who

was a nationwide operation based in Florida, where most of the terrorists lived. John Sugg of the Atlanta weekly *Creative Loafing*, who brought out many of the details of the report, discovered that the Israelis lived on the same street in Hollywood, Florida as Mohammed Atta.

A reliable source told Cameron that "evidence linking these Israelis to 9-11 is classified," which indicates there is evidence. Cameron says that investigators suspect the skyjackers evaded surveillance through Amdocs, Ltd., an Israeli-based telecom firm that has contracts for call records and billing with many American phone companies. Several Israeli art student spies worked for Amdocs and investigators fear that information may have, as Brit Hume put it, "fallen into the wrong hands."

NSA has warned the FBI and CIA about the potential for espionage associated with Amdocs on several occasions.

Another firm, Comverse Infosys, which is a subsidiary of an Israeli telecom company, provides wiretapping software for law enforcement to intercept calls. According to Cameron, the manufacturers have access to the US phone company computers to provide ongoing service, and this access may have "undermined the whole wiretapping system." Comverse works closely with the Israeli Ministry of Industry and Trade, and several former US officials involved in awarding Comverse contracts now work for the company.

---

came in From the Art Sale," *Creative Loafing*, March 20, 2002.

Cameron says that the FBI's CALEA (Communications Assistance for Law Enforcement Act) office is most concerned about the threat, although investigators in New York claim that suspects they sought to tap "immediately changed their telecommunications processes," as if they had been tipped off. This was the case with an Israeli organized crime organization in 1997 that intercepted communications between the LAPD, the FBI, and the Secret Service, and used surveillance of police beepers, cell phones, and home phones to avoid arrest.

We know that Israeli generals have been looking for a green light to attack Palestinian terrorism; their actions since September 11 indicate they received what they wanted. They now have an excuse, the war on terror, to humiliate Arafat, destroy the PLO, and promote a Palestinian civil war. According to Tanya Reinhart of Tel Aviv University, the strategy of generals like Sharon dates to Moshe Dyan's model of grabbing the land and keeping it until the enemy finally gives it to them. This and revenge for suicide bombing explains Israeli motivations behind the direct defensive attacks in the occupied territories in the spring of 2002.

Israel is not immune from indirect defensive attacks. We could almost adopt a prophetic voice, like Isaia in Babylon, and tell you what happened to Lee Harvey Oswald[1] happened to Tim McVeigh—they were given sinister roles after being sheep dipped, that is discharged from the military and covertly

---

[1] His communism was pure fraud, to give one of many examples we could give to illustrate what we mean.

reassigned to intelligence agencies. Something like this happened in case of Rabin's assassination and will happen again in Israel: "An ox knows its owner and an ass its master's manager, but Israel doesn't know, my people haven't understood."[1] Nothing is as it seems; everything is false, most of all the flags upheld by so many covert operations.

23.

Bin Laden, the Saudi skyjackers, and their wealthy financiers find motivation in opposition to US military presence on sacred land where it is writ that two religions should not coexist. They point to contemporary US support for Israel's genocide of Arabs in Palestine and the great betrayal of 1916, sealed in the secret Sykes-Picot agreement, which was only published after the October Revolution in Russia. This agreement concerns the great power partition of the Ottoman Empire after the First World War that contradicted the promises of Arab independence in the Husayn-McMahon correspondence.

It's worth recalling what happened then to find the rational continuity with what is happening now. Ali ibn Husayn was a descendant of the Prophet Muhammad from a prominent

---

[1] Isaia, Book of Judgment 1:1. See Suggest Reading for more sources.

Arabian family, and when the First World War began, he negotiated with Sir Henry McMahon, British high commissioner in Egypt. He would rise against the Turks at the British suggestion and become King of an Arab state, and if all went his way, he could have become Caliph, head of all Muslim peoples, and leader of the Arab nationalist movement that was emerging at that time. Husayn insisted on independence in the Arabian Peninsula, except Aden, and on independence for what are now Iraq, Jordan, Lebanon, and Syria. McMahon replied that except for Baghdad, Basra, and part of the Palestinian coast, Britain recognized and supported the "independence of the Arabs in all the regions within the limits demanded by the Sharif of Mecca."

Husayn began his revolt in 1916, quickly took Mecca and Jeddah, and gave invaluable support to the British advance on Palestine. What did he get in return? Sykes-Picot left Arabia as the only truly independent Arab area and the 1917 Balfour Declaration publicly expressed British support for a Jewish state in Palestine. Although Husayn and his sons had their kingdoms, the elder would lose his title of king of Hejaz to Abd al-Aziz ibn Saoud. The self-proclaimed king of Saudi Arabia subsequently killed his Wahabi followers at the battle of Sabila in 1929 and met with Roosevelt, as mentioned above, paving the way for the eventual US base in Dhahran. Bin Laden despises these betrayals by and concessions to the West and this may be his strongest weapon in the long run. The West would be wise to remember that King Faisal, a strict Wahab unlike his older brother whom he succeeded, was nonetheless assassinated in 1975.

The West views the family line from King Khalid to Crown Prince Fahed as more favorable to its interests than a more fundamentalist regime, which depicts CIA support for extreme Islamic types as asinine. Many sides are played at once in Saudi Arabia, and the United States doesn't have the leverage it did before American companies sold their stake in Aramco to the state in 1988 and before half a million US troops invaded the country during the Gulf War. Resentment runs deep for a wealthy, proud people who naturally despise dependence on foreigners.

24.

Zbiginew Brzezinski, national security advisor under Carter, summarizes the current geopolitical state of world affairs as one of firsts: the first time a single state has true global power, the first time a non-Eurasian state is preeminent, the first time the globe's central arena, Eurasia, is dominated by a non-Eurasian power. The third point would seem to be a liability, at least in the pipeline races, which Zbig, as he is sometimes called, admits must be completed before there can be political stability in the region.

The realistic response to this is to question the risks for pipeline safety in areas that are politically unstable.

Perhaps US bases in Afghanistan will do the trick, but we doubt it. Too many people refuse to be pawns in what Zbig calls *Grand Chessboard*, with its indicative subtitle: "American Primacy and its Geostrategic Imperatives," one of which would be the Ceyhan pipeline project, along with the expansion of NATO to include China, Japan, and several states across Eurasia. The generals and their civilian counterparts have war game boards and tactical plans for every scenario, and we know that these often include the use of pretexts to justify war. For example, Polk sent troops into Mexico in 1846 and said that the ensuing skirmish that spilled American blood justified declaration of war. What amazes us, beyond its sheer lust for dominion, is how much of Brzezinski's analysis and current events found their way into the James Bond film *The World Is Not Enough,* although the villain was mischaracterized as an unfeeling anarchist rather than a suicidal jihadist.

25.

As we contemplate Black Tuesday, we come back to examples of contriving a pretext for war because war has repeatedly been the consequence this of indirect defensive attacks. Statesmen turned a blind eye and offered misdirection in the sinking of the Lusitania, the surprise attack on Pearl Harbor, and the Tonkin Gulf incident, which, respectively, enabled US entry into the First World War, and triggered US entry into the Second World War and the Vietnam War. The Gulf War was no different, which makes Vice President Cheney's evocation of it in his case against foreknowledge of 9-11 particularly hollow.

In his May 19, 2002 appearance on *Meet the Press*, Cheney made the following statement: "We had this in the Gulf War. You may remember the way that got started was with 180,000 Iraqi troops on the border with Kuwait, they invaded Kuwait. Before that, though, everybody, all of our experts, everybody in the region, all the government heads throughout the Mideast said, 'He'll never attack,' and then he did. And you went back after the fact and looked down through the intelligence community and the Department of Defense, for example, and you were able to find one guy who had warned, 'I think he's going to attack.'" We remember reading the reports about Iraqi troop movements and thinking, along with many others, including media pundits, that Saddam Hussein *would* attack. Moreover, we know the administration knew better, including then Secretary of Defense Cheney who said at the time that the United States would defend Kuwait if it were attacked, although the White House downplayed this by saying that Cheney had spoken with "some liberty."[1] The State Department's Margaret Tutweiler expressed the administration's position when she stated that the United States had neither a defense treaty nor security arrangements with Kuwait.

A transcript of the July 29, 1990 meeting between Hussein and US Ambassador to Iraq April Glaspie was later released showing that not only did the United States government know Saddam would invade, but that it offered him an invitation to war. After Saddam restated Iraq's claims on Kuwait, Glaspie replied, "We have no opinion on your Arab-Arab conflicts, such as your dispute with Kuwait. Secretary [of State James] Baker has directed me to emphasize the instruction, first given to Iraq in the 1960s, that the Kuwait issue is not associated with America." Iraq invaded Kuwait on August 2 and on September 2, as she was leaving the embassy, British journalists who had obtained the transcript asked her: "You encouraged this aggression—his invasion. What were you thinking?" Glaspie responded that she didn't think Iraq would "take all of Kuwait" even though she knew that historically it was viewed as part of Iraq.[2] The Gulf War would conclude with the infamous Highway of Death massacre in February 1991 in which the US Air Force killed tens of thousands of retreating Iraqi soldiers. Subsequent sanctions against Iraq resulted in innumerable deaths from disease,

---

[1] Stephanie Reich, "Slow Motion Holocaust: U.S. Designs on Iraq," *Covert Action Quarterly* (spring, 2002), 25.
[2] Jim Keith, ed. *Secret and Suppressed* (Portland, 1993), 181–2.

especially among children, as predicted by the Defense Intelligence Agency.[1]

Was the War on Terrorism launched by a similarly deceptive tactic, by allowing an attack to take place so as to beat it back? Will the war be fought, as the war in Afghanistan suggests by the early massacres, with equal disregard for civilian life? Or is everything as it appears to be when the vice president joins Leno on Late Night or when the president's spokesperson speaks to the press corps? They wouldn't lie, would they?

We ask these questions because it is always prudent to imagine a worst case scenario and because we have read reports of seemingly insane ruses. One planned stratagem was a reckless plot reportedly dreamed up on the pretext of a prearranged, limited nuclear exchange with the Soviet Union. Whistleblower Al Martin claims in *The Conspirators* to have attended a meeting where this was discussed with the principals, with chilling details, such as mass arrests and jailing.[2]

We don't know if this happened, but given what we know about Operation Northwoods, nothing is, as Vice President Cheney says, beyond the pale. We have read horrid allegations that plutonium was found in Iraq after the massacre in the Gulf. With this in mind and Bush's Wolfowitzian speech at West Point in the summer of 2002 about the use of first strike tactics against a host of nations, we ask international inspectors to determine

---

[1] Reich, "Slow Motion Holocaust," 25.
[2] Al Martin, *The Conspirators* (Pray, 2002), 338.

whether tactical nuclear bombs were used in Afghanistan. The mushroom clouds over Tora Bora and our strategic outlook force us imagine the worst.

Terrorism, which fails as a long-term strategy for small groups with big demands, can be an effective if messy tactic when used defensively by states. In *Lessons of Terror*,[1] Caleb Carr makes a breezy case that manumission of slaves was what lead to the longevity of Rome and that the destruction of Carthage in the Third Punic War was the beginning of Rome's downfall. We're somewhat surprised to read this interpretation from a military historian who should know that it was precisely Rome's predatory wars in the Mediterranean and slavery that transformed it from a small city-state into a world power. Indemnities were collected after the First and Second Punic Wars and tremendous booty was seized by Roman commanders in Greece and Macedonia. The capture of Spanish mines ensured ample silver for coinage. Slaves poured into Rome from captured territories—some 25,000 from Agrigentum; 20,000 from Carthage; and 30,000 from Tarentum during the First Punic War. When the cities of Epirus were routed in 167 B.C., 150,000 people were sold as slaves. All of Carthage's inhabitants who hadn't been killed were enslaved when the city was razed in sixteen-day fire—a Carr example of

---

[1] Caleb Carr, *Lessons of Terror* (New York, 2002), 19–20.

the failed terrorist tactics. The sowing of Carthaginian fields with salt kept Rome's main rival down never to rise again.

The contents of Carr's book do not match its expansive subtitle, "A History of Warfare Against Civilians: Why It Has Always Failed and Why It Will Fail Again," because many instances of American state terrorism, with the exception of Vietnam, were successes: from the wars against the First Nations to the use of Contras in Nicaragua and beyond.

We come to the conclusion that we need not fear terrorism, suicide bombings and the like, when they are offensive, beyond requisite precautions for personal safety. Make no mistake about it, all precautions must be taken against offensive terrorism, but these terrorist operations will never win over the population and transform a society. When terrorism is defensive and designed to gain sympathy for the state, out of fear, or to instill fear of the state in the population, we are right to be afraid and dismiss accusations that our suspicions are paranoid.

The most illustrative and tragic example of this is the way the state appears to have sponsored the assassination of Martin Luther King Jr., according to two excellently executed books: *Orders to Kill* by William F. Pepper and *Murder in Memphis* by Mark Lane and Dick Gregory. King's police protection was removed on the fateful day, April 4, 1968, and the FBI team directed to "destroy" King conveniently investigated the murder. We could mention more details, such as King's incisive demands for jobs, housing, and civil rights, but our main point, and on this we are certain, is that this assassination was designed as the defensive use of terror—*indirectly* to prompt blacks to look to the state for protection if they had been deceived or *directly* to keep blacks quiet, out of fear, if they knew.

We've made a strong case for the state-terror thesis as it applies to 9-11 because time and again terrorists and their financiers were abetted by the state and the public deceived. Even several FBI agents—careful readers remember the names Coleen Rowley and Robert Wright, to which we can add the improbable name Tyrone Powers[1]—have made these allegations. If our assertions are proved wrong, we will stand corrected. But until then, having demonstrated their contribution to the events, we must speculate on the comparative negligence of states and statesmen. Was it 90 percent, 80 percent? We'll settle for 50 percent and toast the lawyer in *The Fall* by Camus who recognized his guilt in every judgment.

Morals aside, we must see the minutes of Energy Task Force meetings and know what was being said about Afghanistan and Central Asia. Nothing should be redacted out for national security reasons because that is simply too convenient a cover for statesmen who should pay for their misdeeds and who probably never wrote anything down about the operation, for obvious

---

[1] We say improbable because this deceased actor's name signifies for us the former FBI special agent who says Bush knew in advance. Dennis Shipman, "Another Spook Who Sat Behind the Door," *Black World Today*, July 9, 2002.

reasons.[1] We need to find out more about how Enron was engaged in negotiations with the Taliban using Saudi Prince Turki, then chief of intelligence, as an intermediary. Was the National Security Council or the Energy Task Force meeting on methods to rescue Enron, including, among other things, stock options and insider trading that bet for the terrorists and on a gas pipeline through Afghanistan, after the preplanned war, to India?

If so, this would have been for Enron's failing $3 billion Dabhol energy plant. We know, for example, that Vice President Cheney pushed the Maharashtra State Electricity Board to pay its debts to Enron at a June 27 meeting with Sonia Gandhi.[2] We also know that President Bush was to mention the issue with Indian Prime Minister Vajpayee, but the idea was reportedly dropped.

We recall that Enron was the biggest contributor to the Bush-Cheney 2000 election campaign and that the company conducted a feasibility study for a $2.5 billion trans-Caspian gas pipeline based on a joint venture agreement singed in February 1999 between Turkmenistan, Bechtel, and General Electric Capital Services. Enron has had a stake in developing Uzbekistan's natural gas fields since 1996; Unocal and Enron invited the Taliban to Sugarland, Texas, in late 1997, to pitch a

---

[1] A Department of Energy lawyer working on the Task Force documents tells us nothing is in them that would support our thesis.

[2] The plant was built but never used. Enron's partners were General Electric and Bechtel. Timothy J. Burger, "Veep Tried to Aid Enron: Key Role in India debt row," *Daily News*, January 18, 2002.

136

pipeline deal; the visit is described in a poignant way by Ahmed Rashid's indispensable *Taliban*.

We assert that oil and gas pipelines through Afghanistan were high on Bush's primary foreign agenda. We can't fail to note that Halliburton, where Cheney was CEO when he argued for more open trade with nations sponsoring terrorism,[1] is one of the foremost pipeline builders in the world through its subsidiary Brown and Root. The United States has already sent advisors to Georgia and Uzbekistan to train intelligence units in pipeline safety.

In the chapter entitled "The World Crisis and Its Various Manifestations" of his *Real Report*, Sanguinetti diverts a formulation by the economist Ricardo and asserts it is not wheat but oil that "can be defined as the necessary and indispensable product to produce and consume all others." With so much lucre at stake for oil and gas, and so many people in the current administration so fixated on them, we should not be surprised, given so many historical precedents, by the use of a pretext to wage war with Afghanistan. What is surprising is how this could happen, that the representatives of big oil would take power and roll over everyone in their way, without the masses figuring out what had happened. In an article entitled "Afghan Pipeline Given Go-Ahead," the BBC tells us on May 30, 2002, "The leaders of Afghanistan, Pakistan and Turkmenistan have agreed to construct

---

[1] Center for Public Integrity, August 2000 cited in Molly Ivins, "What took so long?" Creators Syndicate, June 6, 2002.

a $2 billion pipeline to bring gas from Central Asia to the sub-continent. The project was abandoned in 1998," the article says, although we now know that talks continued under other guises, "when a consortium led by US energy company Unocal withdrew from the project over fears of being seen to support Afghanistan's then Taliban government.[1] The three countries have agreed to invite international tenders and guarantee funding before launching the project. Unocal has repeatedly denied it is interested in returning to Afghanistan despite having conducted the original feasibility study to build the pipeline. The pipeline could eventually supply gas to India."

If these pipelines were the real goal, then 9-11 was a deceptive event, like the other staged pretexts, lures, and indirect defensive attakcs we've examined above that only occasionally, and then momentarily, look bad for leaders who have learned to make tragic events work for them by using more false threats and attacks. Ruses have been used since ancient times and amount to nothing less than the secret art of war. In rare instances, such as 9-11, the public's desire for the truth about hidden activity wins out because the sacrifice for a stratagem was too great. We will find out, if justice is done, who in the Bush administration and who else profited on Wall Street from inside knowledge of the attacks of September 11. Who is on the SEC's Insider Trading Control List?

---

[1] Feminists were instrumental in bringing about the company's reassessment.

138

Unfortunately, we will probably never know what information NSA had on insider trades prior to 9-11 because, according to Tom Flocco,[1] NSA lawyers are insisting that they cannot collect data on Americans, although former officials counter that information can be preserved on US citizens if it pertains to a foreign intelligence operation. We already have the case of FBI agents Jeffrey Royer and Lynn Wingate being indicted for allegedly giving information to Amr Elgindy[2] and his associates Derrick Cleveland and Troy Peters. Elgindy, who allegedly had access to confidential law enforcement databases, called his broker on September 10 to sell stocks while predicting a crash.[3]

If congressional investigators wished to sort out what happened around 9-11, they would hire former LAPD detective Michael Ruppert who knows how Wall Street and the major banks are linked to the CIA. Ruppert and investigative reporter Tom Flocco have been on the case of Deutsche Bank's suspicious pre-attack trades and connections to CIA Executive Director Buzzy Krongard.[4] At the UnansweredQuestions press conference, Flocco tied Deutsche Bank to Enron's special purpose entities and suspicious deletions and destruction of documents made under the direction of a former SEC

---

[1] Unanswered Questions inaugural press conference.
[2] Alternately, Amr El Gindy.
[3] n.a., "FBI Agents Indicted in Insider Trading Ring," Reuters, May 22, 2002.
[4] Michael Ruppert, "Evidence of Criminal Insider Trading Leads Directly into Highest Levels of CIA," *From the Wilderness*, October 9, 2001.

enforcement director. What Flocco has also done is obtain the names of the thirty-eight firms the SEC asked Canadian securities officials about and compared them with the financial records of the top hundred Bush administration officials and discovered they owned millions of dollars in these stocks. All of these circumstances appear against the backdrop of what could be $15 billion in insider trading deals.

We will discover, if justice is carried out, who profited from heroin scare tactics against the Taliban and who is profiting from the latest Afghan opium harvest,[1] banned by the Taliban, and what former and even active duty CIA officers were doing in the poppy and oil fields of Uzbekistan and for Enron in the summer of 2001.[2] We wouldn't normally turn to *National Enquirer* but they have Atul Davda, once senior director for Enron's International Division on the record: "Enron had intimate contact with Taliban officials. Building the pipeline was one of the corporation's prime objectives." And the paper has the State Department's press officer for South Asian Affairs, Len Scensny, on the record confirming the Taliban visit to oil companies in Sugarland, Texas, namely Enron and Unocal.

---

[1] Brian Downing Quig, "Is the United States About to Attack Afghanistan Because It Shut Off the Heroin?" *True Democracy*, Fall 2001 and Michael Ruppert, "The Lies About Taliban Heroin, CIA Seizes Control of Drug Trade: Russia and Oil the Real Objectives with Heroin as a Weapon of War," *From the Wilderness*, October 11, 2001.

[2] Alan Bernstein, "The fall of Enron: Security team leaves Enron to form firm," *Houston Chronicle*, January 23, 2002, A13; n.a., "Enron Gave Taliban Millions," *National Enquirer*, March 4, 2002 and n.a., "Enron: The Untold Story," *National Enquirer*, February 15, 2002.

140

The *National Enquirer* has made several assertions attributed variously to congressional, FBI, and CIA sources. The most startling are that "Enron secretly employed active CIA agents to carry out its dealings overseas," and that Enron gained information from the intelligence satellite project Echelon to "land billions of lucrative contracts overseas." We were also astounded to learn that "When Clinton was bombing Bin Laden camps in Afghanistan in 1998, Enron was making payoffs to Taliban and Bin Laden operatives to keep the pipeline project alive." The last remark, attributed to an FBI source, went on to say, "And there's no way that anyone could NOT have known of the Taliban and Bin Laden connection at that time, especially Enron who had CIA agents on its payroll!"

If justice comes into balance, the world will discover the military and paramilitary men who profited from the death of thousands of their fellow citizens. We have to be open to the idea that how the soldier, as we quoted Machiavelli in our preface, "in his work—if he wants to make a steady profit from it—must be rapacious, fraudulent, violent, and exhibit many qualities that, of necessity, do not make him good." If justice reigns, we will find out who murdered Enron executive Cliff Baxter in January 2002 before he could speak about dirty dealing in Sugarland.[1]

---

[1] David Wright, Kevin Lynch, and Courtney Callahan, "Baxter's Suicide Was Murder Say Top Cops," *National Enquirer*, March 4, 2002.

26.

The indications that the United States provoked a
preemptive strike and allowed it to happen to advance energy,
construction, and military interests are as follows: 1) the United
States threatened the Taliban with a military overthrow and
return of the king in exile if, among other conditions, a pipeline
deal could not be negotiated; 2) the United States knew many if
not all of the skyjacking suspects, had trailed them, and may have
trained some of them at Pensacola Naval Air Station; 3) the
United States granted visas to many of the skyjackers at the
consular office in Jeddah, which has been overrun by the CIA for
many years; 4) the United States received specific warnings about
the attacks, which it in turn relayed or registered in several ways;
5) some FBI agents were thwarted by politicians and other
bureaucrats from preventing the attacks; 6) the military response
to the attacks on September 11, as demonstrated in our timeline,
was highly suspicious; 7) the Bush family ties with the bin Laden
family—allowed to leave the country without being questioned
after the attacks—at a time when both families were members of
the large defense industry company, Carlyle Group, which
happens to provide extensive training for Saudi defense forces;

and 8) the CIA's ties with Pakistan's Inter-Services Intelligence in creating the Taliban and the long anti-Soviet struggle must be seen in the light of the traitorous Kunduz Airlift on November 25.

Lest we forget, it's worth recalling the Kunduz incident: in an area controlled by the Northern Alliance, CIA, and Delta Force, a scenario unfolded whereby Pakistani advisors dashed for planes and brought Taliban and al-Qaeda leadership with them. Thousands were flown to safety in Pakistan with the apparent approval of the United States, although officials deny the airlift took place. Bitter soldiers will tell resentful tales as to why the enemy got away.

On the morning of September 11, Representative Goss (R-Fla.) and Senator Graham (D-Fla.), who now lead the Joint Inquiry investigation, were having breakfast in the Capitol with the head of the Pakistan's Inter-Services Intelligence, General Mahmood Ahmed, a man now under arrest for abetting head terrorist Atta with $100,000 in the summer of 2001. In case you missed this one, Indian intelligence, in leaks to the *Times of India*, says it supplied the FBI with a number that enabled intercepts of between General Mahmood Ahmed and a known terrorist, Ahmed Omar Sheikh pertaining to the wiring of $100,000 from Pakistan to the US bank account of Mohammed Atta.[1]

---

[1] Wayne Madsen, "Afghanistan, the Taliban and the Bush Oil Team," Centre for Research on Globalisation, January 23, 2002, 7–8.

The Democratic senator from Indiana, Evan Bayh, has already remarked that the Joint Inquiry Committee somehow found no smoking gun when guns smoke all over the place.[1] What about the FAA report of a gunshot on skyjacked American Airlines flight 11, or Baxter's suspicious suicide, or the surface-to-air guns with rotating turrets on the White House and Pentagon that failed to fire? What about the report from Evan Thomas in *Newsweek* (September 24, 2001) that on September 10 high-ranking Defense Department officials were advised to cancel travel plans for the morning of September 11 for security reasons?

If a truly independent and honest commission is formed, it will have to look for traces of evidence that have been destroyed or covered-up and account for witnesses who have been killed. Men like Thomas Kelly, the FBI lawyer known to have obstructed the congressional Waco investigation, should automatically be excluded from the process.[2] We hope someone, some brave statesman or woman who can name names will come clean on 9-11. It's not likely because people with power are lining up with the victor, such as the federal judge hearing wrongful death cases from the victim's families who granted the Justice Department the right to review and keep secret information

---

[1] Dana Priest and Juliet Eilperin, "Panel Finds No 'Smoking Gun' in Probe of 9/11 Intelligence Failures," *Washington Post*, July 11, 2002, 1.

[2] Richard Leiby and Dana Priest, "Head of Sept. 11 Probe Allegedly Obstructed Danforth's Waco Inquiry," *Washington Post*, June 22, 2002, 6.

dealing with national security.[1] No matter how much one dirty hand washes the other, the fingers of statesmen who authored and covered up the attacks by turning a blind eye and by misdirection remain stained with blood and oil.

[1] Diego Ibarguen, "Judge Grants Government a Role in Sept. 11 Wrongful Death Lawsuits," Associated Press, July 12, 2002.

II.

Amerithrax Attack

"He who wishes to snatch advantage takes a devious and distant route and makes it the short way. He turns misfortune to his advantage. He deceives and fools the enemy to make him dilatory and lax, and then marches on speedily."

Sun Tzu, *Art of War*

We take the name for this chapter from the FBI case because of the poetic justice expressed in this neologism. The anthrax-laced letters sent through the US Postal service in the weeks following Black Tuesday were less deadly but perhaps more disturbing than other nefarious episodes leading to the war on terror because they were clearly authored by a fellow citizen or more than one—a conspiracy. The attacks and subsequent investigation, we will show, support the state-terror thesis.

The research, manufacture, and deployment of weapons grade anthrax has been exclusively the purview of government labs for the last half century. The individuals possessing skill and equipment to produce such a weapon have almost all been, at one time or another, either directly or indirectly employed by the government. The US government has a history of ignoring or defying international attempts to regulate or ban the research and development of biological warfare agents, including anthrax. The choice of targets and timing of the attacks both point to statesmen and state agencies.

Producing anthrax in a form that can be used as a weapon is a difficult and dangerous procedure. Although the initial anthrax letters made it easy for nonstate agents to perpetuate hundreds of hoaxes, most notably those of anti-abortion fugitive Clayton Lee Wagner, the limited deployment of actual anthrax letters is an indication of the difficulty of working with the deadly bacteria. This limited scope is also an indication that the perpetrators had specific goals that could be achieved with a small operation.

US government research into how best to use anthrax as a weapon began at Camp, later Fort, Detrick, Maryland in 1943.[1] The work included developing the most potent strains of the bug, and producing those strains in the best form for use as a weapon. Scientists at the US Army Medical Research Institute for Infectious Diseases (USAMRIID) at Fort Detrick succeeded in producing a strain of anthrax so powerful that a single gallon of the bacteria contained up to eight billion lethal doses, more than enough to kill every human being on the planet.[2] Producing the bug in a manner that could be distributed, "weaponizing it", is more difficult. The preferred method of deployment as a weapon

---

[1] Judith Miller et. al., *Germs*, (New York, 2001) 39.
[2] Ibid., 35.

is aerosol; in the anthrax attacks of 2001, the inhaled anthrax spores proved far more deadly than the ones that attacked their victims through the skin.

Anthrax bacteria can exist in two states. In its active state it is a microscopic, rod-shaped bacteria, small enough to bypass the natural defenses of the human respiratory tract. In this state, a few, deadly bacteria will quickly multiply to millions in the warm, moist environment of the human body. It is also fragile and difficult to work with in its active state. The process of making the bacteria hardy and stable enough for use in an aerosol, or delivery in an ordinary postal envelope, is much more difficult. The facilities required for this procedure exceed even well-equipped state or commercial biotechnology laboratories.

The scientists at Fort Detrick found that they could produce anthrax in its second form, its dormant state, as a spore. This form is both hardier and easier to work with, though still deadly. Using heat and chemical shock, the scientists could transform the bacteria into its spore state near the end of its growth cycle. Done correctly, the spores can resist heat, disinfectants, sunlight, and more. Upon being inhaled, the spores return to their active state and infect the host.[1]

The anthrax in letters sent to Democratic Senators Daschle and Leahy, respectively majority leader and chairman of the Judiciary Committee, was the highest grade found in the attacks.

---

[1] Ibid., 39.

This anthrax was prepared in the manner typical of US military processes: the particles had a very narrow size range, and were treated to eliminate static charges so as not to clump but float in the air. The U.S. weaponization process is secret, but we understand it requires a combination of chemicals and at least five patented processes. A coating found on the spores was typical of secret US government processes.[1]

A few dozen individuals in the United States have the ability to produce anthrax spores in such a dense concentration. Of the facilities known to have worked with the bacteria, only four laboratories in the United States could produce anthrax of this quality. David Franz, a former United Nations weapons inspector in Iraq and biodefense scientist at USAMRIID, stated, "Only a very small group of people could have made this… If you look at the sample from the standpoint of biology, it tells me this person [who made the anthrax] was very good at what they do. And this wasn't the first batch they've made. They've done this for years. The concentration was a trillion spores [of anthrax] per gram. That's incredibly concentrated."[2]

In 1972, the Biological and Toxin Weapons Convention, a treaty prohibiting the possession of deadly biological agents except for research into defensive measures, was signed by London, Washington, and Moscow, and opened for signature by

---

[1] Barbara Rosenberg, *Analysis of the Anthrax Attacks* (SUNY-Purchase, February 5, 2002), 5.
[2] Laura Rozen, "Is a U.S. bioweapons scientist behind last fall's anthrax attacks?," *Salon.com*, February 8, 2002, 1.

the United Nations. The treaty would eventually be signed by more than one hundred and forty other nations and go into effect in March 1975. This was the first time a treaty banned an entire class of weapons, but it was so weak and full of loopholes that it was almost immediately violated. Work at Fort Detrick continued.

Attempts to introduce protocols aimed at enforcement of the treaty have been consistently resisted by signatories, especially the US government. As recently as mid-2001, the Bush administration announced opposition to new language allowing for proposed enforcement of the treaty. Almost all other signatories, including close US allies Britain and Japan, supported the protocol, and criticized the Bush administration for its unilateralism. After the fall of the Soviet Union and the apartheid regime in South Africa, the United States, apparently stands alone among industrialized nations in its desire to pursue biological warfare development programs.

A great deal of research into biological warfare agents can be made in the name of defending civilians and military personnel against potential attacks. One such line of research has been the creation of a vaccine against anthrax. By the 1980s research into vaccines in the commercial sector had slowed to a near standstill, owing to the expense, the risk of lawsuits, and low returns of this type of research. Drug companies prefer to research drugs to treat a disease rather than vaccines to prevent it, and at any rate, the market for an anthrax vaccine would be, at most, tiny.

151

Pentagon biowarfare studies concluded that the military needed to protect soldiers against anthrax with a vaccine. One had been developed in the fifties, and although the vaccine was several decades old, it had rarely been used, and was still somewhat experimental. The vaccine was considered likely to cause reactions and unlikely to protected against all strains. Only one laboratory in the United States, at the Michigan Department of Public Health in Lansing, manufactured the vaccine.

At this point, a corporation with deep ties to the military establishment and the Republican party, purchased the laboratory producing a vaccine with almost no market. According to their own website, the BioPort corporation was "Founded in 1998 for the sole purpose of acquiring the assets of the Michigan Biologic Products Institute from the State of Michigan."[1] BioPort was essentially founded to create the anthrax vaccine. The assets of Michigan Biologics Products were acquired September 4, 1998, less than a month before the Pentagon would order its historic purchase of large quantities of anthrax vaccine.

BioPort produces the only FDA licensed anthrax vaccine, and this is practically its only product. As of this writing, all of this vaccine is manufactured for and purchased by the Department of Defense. Although BioPort has obtained FDA approval to manufacture the vaccine for the public, all of the vaccine it has the capacity to produce is owned by the US

---

[1] www.bioport.com.

military. The connections of BioPort to the White House include US Navy Admiral Richard Crowe, chairman of the Joint Chiefs of Staff under Bush the Elder's administration, who sits on the board with a thirteen percent share. Chief Executive Officer Fuad El-Habri and other executives of BioPort are all large contributors to the Republican Party and the presidential campaign of George W. Bush.

On September 29, 1988, the army signed its first-ever contract to purchase large quantities of the vaccine, a contract for three hundred thousand doses.[1] Because the vaccine was administered in six doses spread out over eighteen months, the three hundred thousand doses were enough to protect fifty thousand soldiers. The first time large numbers of soldiers were asked to take the vaccine was during the Gulf War against Iraq in 1991. In violation of standard medical procedures for, what were at the time, unproved medications, no informed consent, nor waiver of informed consent, was obtained from service members at the time of the Gulf War, and none was sought from the FDA.

Those few soldiers who refused the vaccine faced reprisals. As reported in the *Washington Post*, "more than 400 members of the military opt(ed) to quit or be court-martialed rather than roll up their sleeves," for the potentially hazardous vaccine.[2] Texas National Guard CPT Jody Grenge, who served nearly 18 years as

---

[1] Judith Miller et. al. *Germs* (New York, 2001), 87.
[2] Rick Weiss, "Demand Growing For Anthrax Vaccine: Fear of Bioterrorism Attack Spurs Requests for Controversial Shot," *Washington Post*, September 29, 2001, A16.

153

a medical operation officer, was forced out of her position for refusing the anthrax vaccine on religious grounds, in addition to a history of adverse reactions to vaccinations.[1] Nine pilots of the 103rd Fighter Wing of the Connecticut Air National Guard were forced to resign after refusing an order not to talk to the press about their misgivings concerning the Pentagon's use of the vaccine.

More than thirty pilots and 17 KC-10 tanker crew members at Travis Air Force Base in California quit instead of taking the vaccine. Captain John Buck, an emergency room physician at Kessler Air Force Base in Mississippi, became the first military doctor to be court-martialed for refusing to administer the anthrax vaccine. He is being charged with disobeying an order, but, because of reasons of medical ethics, Buck believes the order to administer the vaccine is an "unlawful order" under the Uniform Code of Military Justice. In an interview with MilitaryCorruption.com, Buck stated, "Informed consent must be part of this program," and that his goal was for, "the program to be made voluntary, or get rid of it altogether."[2] A study commissioned by the Canadian Department of National Defense, and published on their website, found a significant relationship between receiving bio-warfare vaccines and Gulf War Syndrome.[3] A British study found that for both Gulf War and Bosnian War

---

[1] Maj. Glenn MacDonald, USAR (ret), "Greed and Guinea Pigs: Risking the Health of the U.S. Military," www.militarycorruption.com, 2000.

[2] Ibid.

[3] www.dnd.ca/menu/press/reports/health/healthstudyeng1.htm.

veterans there was a correlation between receiving the anthrax vaccine and symptoms consistent with Gulf War Syndrome.[1] Coincidentally, on the same day the Pentagon ordered its vaccine, September 29, 1988, eleven strains of germs, including four types of anthrax (one of which, strain 11966, had been developed at Fort Detrick) were shipped from the American Type Culture Collection in Maryland to Iraq.[2] Yes, to Iraq.

The strain used in the attacks in 2001 has been genetically traced to a strain developed by government scientists at Fort Detrick. Substantial genetic differences can emerge in anthrax bacteria that has been separated for as few as three years, making it highly unlikely that this strain of anthrax came from a source outside the lab.[3]

The chronology of the anthrax attacks, and their relation to the administration's reaction to September 11, demonstrated a cynical use of the politics of terrorism. The anthrax letters mailed to Tom Brokaw at NBC Nightly News and to the *New York Post* were postmarked in Trenton, NJ on September 18, one week after the 9-11 attacks. Whoever grew the anthrax at Fort Detrick was prepared in advance of September 11 to mail the letters. NBC failed to recognize the danger of the brown granular material in the letter.

---

[1] C. Unwin et al, "Health of UK Servicemen Who Served in the Persian Gulf War," *Lancet* 1999, 353:169–178.
[2] Judith Miller et. al. *Germs* (New York, 2001), 89.
[3] Debora MacKenzie, "Anthrax Attack Bug 'Identical' to Army Strain," *NewScientist.com*, May 9, 2002.

Hoax letters mailed to NBC and the New York Post were mailed on September 20 from St. Petersburg, Florida. These false strikes were most likely part of the same initial attack— we say this because the first reports by the media were not until October 12, after the letters sent to Senators Daschle and Leahy.

Another letter was mailed in late September that links the killer to USAMRIID. This letter was sent to Quantico Marine Base in Northern Virginia and accused a former USAMRIID scientist named Dr. Asaad of being a terrorist. It was a long, typewritten letter demonstrating a good command of the English language and in-depth knowledge of Dr. Asaad's personal life and his work at USAMRIID, although it contained a few factual errors. Dr. Asaad would be exonerated by the FBI. This letter was sent before any cases of anthrax occurred.

The anthrax letters to Senators Daschle and Leahy were mailed on October 9, and although these letters were similar to the media letters in many ways, the anthrax was much finer, less granular. The letters sent to NBC Nightly News in September may have simply encountered moisture during the delivery process, or the terrorist may have had time to further weaponize the anthrax used in the later letters. At any rate, all three poison letters to the senators and Brokaw were postmarked from Trenton, NJ, and the FBI believes it is "highly probable, bordering on certainty, that all three letters were authored by the same person."[1]

The first report of an anthrax case came in Florida on October 4, although the information was not released to the media. At this point no link to any suspicious letters was made, and authorities insisted the contamination was accidental, possibly from an animal. The Florida victim, an editor for the Boca Raton *Sun*, died on October 5. The same day, hoax letters were mailed to the *New York Times* and the *St. Petersburg Times*. When the Daschle and Leahy letters were sent from Trenton on October 9, no reports of anthrax mailings had yet been made in the media, although in the wake of September 11, concern arose among specialists about the origin of the anthrax cases.

By October 9 the attacker had mailed all the letters that would be used in the attack, including hoax letters that could credibly have come from the same source. It was not until October 12 and 13 that reports surfaced in the media regarding the NBC anthrax case and the suspicious letters at NBC and the *New York Post*. The weeks following September 11 were busy ones for the Bush administration and the military and intelligence communities. Efforts were being made to pursue a war in Afghanistan and around the world, and to enact sweeping reforms at home which would culminate in the June 2002

---

[1]   FBI Critical Incidence Response Group, National Center for the Analysis of Violent Crime, Amerithrax Press Briefing (Washington, DC, November 9, 2001), 1.

proposal to Congress for a new Cabinet-level department, the Department of Homeland Security.

Less than a week after the quadruple skyjackings, sweeping anti-terrorism legislation was introduced. One reason for the speed of the introduction was that many of its once controversial measures had been introduced in previous legislation and rejected by a narrowly divided Congress. In the climate of fear produced by the hijackings and anthrax attacks, the Patriot Act was overwhelmingly passed.

The anti-terror bill was proposed to an initially skeptical Congress on September 16. Two days later the NBC and *New York Post* letters were mailed from Trenton, New Jersey. On September 28, a case of anthrax at NBC was reported in a boy who had been visiting the network. A few days later, on October 2, the USA Patriot Act was formally introduced in Congress.

Senate Majority Leader Thomas Daschle maintained his cool and stated on October 3 that the Senate should not hurry to enact the sweeping Patriot Act legislation. An angry Attorney General John Ashcroft accused the Democrats of moving too slowly. Senator Patrick Leahy, chairman of the Senate Judiciary Committee, October 4 warned of potential constitutional flaws in the law enforcement legislation. There was growing concern that the act was a threat to liberty.

The editor of the tabloid Boca Raton *Sun* died on October 5. On October 9, Senate Democrats blocked an attempt to rush the Patriot Act to a vote with little debate and no time for amendments. The same day identical letters with high-grade anthrax almost certainly produced at Fort Detrick were mailed to Senators Daschle and Leahy.

On October 11 the Senate and House passed their versions of the bill, and it went to conference the next day as a second anthrax case was reported at NBC offices in Manhattan. Bush claimed on October 13 that the anthrax letter may have been linked to bin Laden and al-Qaeda. A letter with Islamic threats and phrases was opened by Tom Brokaw on October 15 and the next day, Senate office buildings were shut down from fear of anthrax contamination. A day after that, on October 17, House buildings were shut down for the same reason. Dan Rather's assistant contracted anthrax on October 18. By October 25, all Congressional mail was halted and on October 26, as soon as the Senate passed the final version, President Bush signed the Patriot Act into law.

The choice of targets is at least as revealing as the chronology. The media targets seem to have been chosen in order to sow fear across a broad spectrum of the American public. Both tabloid and more mainstream newspapers were targets, although the attacker seemed to have had some difficulty getting the correct addresses for the tabloid newspapers. All of the main television network news divisions received actual anthrax or hoax letters, we surmise, because most Americans get their news from television.

The choice of the senators attacked is somewhat less obvious. Senator Daschle, as Majority Leader of a Senate that only came under Democratic control with the post-Bush election defection of Vermont Senator James Jeffords, was the leader of the loyal opposition to the administration. The Supreme Court decided election of President Bush and the Jeffords defection, made the political stakes in the Senate very high indeed.

A single Senate seat meant the difference in control of committee chairmanships, and control of which bills would make it to the floor. Even with the rallying cry of a "war on terrorism" and President Bush riding high in the opinion polls, the Democrats had everything to gain by pressing hard against the White House agenda.

Senate Judiciary Committee Chairman, Vermont Senator Patrick Leahy was in a position to delay any legislation regarding domestic law enforcement policy and spending. Oversight of the Justice Department and its key bureau, the FBI, came under his purview. Daschle and Leahy were the Democratic leadership that could potentially stand in the way of the White House agenda on domestic policing that will eventually be realized with the Department of Homeland Security.

These two targets had almost no value for a foreign Islamist terrorist organization. Only a domestic agenda could possibly be pursued by threatening these two powerful individuals. Whoever sent these letters must have been concerned about the balance of power on Capitol Hill, especially about the oversight of the

Senate Judiciary Committee on domestic police budgets and policy.

The FBI, in its profile of the Amerithrax suspect, states he "did not select victims randomly. He made an effort to identify the correct address, including zip code, of each victim and used sufficient postage to ensure proper delivery of the letters. The offender deliberately selected NBC News, the *New York Post*, and the office of Senator Tom Daschle as the targeted victims (and possibly AMI in Florida). These targets are probably very important to the offender."[1]

The FBI has acknowledged that the perpetrator of the anthrax attacks is probably a domestic terrorist, without a likely link to Islamists such as al-Qaeda. As early as November 9, 2001, when the FBI released a profile of the Amerithrax suspect, it acknowledged the individual was probably not a member of a foreign terrorist cell, but more likely a technician living in the United States. As recently as June 13, 2002, in an interview with Associated Press reporters, anonymous Federal law enforcement officials stated that the anthrax used in the attacks was actually grown at Fort Detrick.[2]

Credible reports that the anthrax attacks came from within the US biological warfare establishment were made as early as November, 2001. Reuters news service reported on November

---

[1] Ibid.
[2] Ted Bridis, "FBI Probes Leads on Anthrax Source," Associated Press, June 14, 2002.

28, 2001 that a member of the US delegation to the United Nations, speaking in Berlin, believed the anthrax attacks were an "inside job." Reuters reported that the delegation had information that had not been made public.[1]

Consider the strange case of Dr. Steven J. Hatfill, a former Fort Detrick biowarfare researcher who still lives just outside the gates of the Frederick, Maryland complex. Dr. Hatfill, at 48 years of age, is a colorful character with an unusual background and a long time interest in biowarfare. He is a physician and Ph.D., a pilot with special training in aviation and submarine medicine who has completed Army Special Forces training. He spent fourteen months as a researcher in Antarctica, and told his college alumni magazine he completed United Nations training to become a bioweapons inspector in Iraq. More importantly, throughout his career he has maintained a special interest in the use of anthrax as a weapon.

He attended medical school in Zimbabwe, then known as Rhodesia. Laura Rozen, of *American Prospect*, reports that, "From 1975-1978, he served with the US Army Institute for Military Assistance, based in Fort Bragg, North Carolina, while simultaneously, his resume says, serving in the Special Air Squadron (SAS) of the white supremacist regime in Rhodesia."[2] He has described in 1979-1980 the largest known outbreak of

---

[1] n.a. "Report: US Expert Believed Behind Anthrax Attacks," Reuters (Berlin, November 28, 2001), 1.

[2] Laura Rozen, "Who is Steven Hatfill," The American Prospect Online, June 20, 2002.

human anthrax, some 10,000 cases. Scott Shane of the *Baltimore Sun* notes that, "Experts still debate whether the Zimbabwe outbreak occurred naturally or was a tactic in the civil war then raging between the white government and black guerillas."[1] While in Rhodesia, Dr. Hatfill lived a few miles from a Greendale School. The return address of one of the Amerithrax letters was of a fictitious "Greendale School" in New Jersey.

Hatfill was hired at USAMRIID in 1997, where he worked until leaving in 1999 to go to the defense contractor Scientific Applications International Corporation while still maintaining privileges at USAMRIID. His security clearance was suspended by the Department of Defense on August 23, 2001, yet restored in March, 2002. In 1997, Dr. Hatfill told *Washington Times* columnist Fred Reed it would not be hard to mount a biological attack. The next year he was photographed for *Insight* magazine demonstrating how to create a batch of plague in a kitchen using common household ingredients and protective gear from a supermarket. Like other biowarfare scientists, Dr. Hatfill has received the anthrax vaccine.

In 1999 Dr. Hatfill commissioned a study describing a potential terrorist attack using an envelope containing weapons grade anthrax. The study was written by Dr. Hatfill's mentor, coworker at SAIC and godfather of the US biowarfare program William C. Patrick III. It describes the danger of anthrax spores

---

[1] Scott Shane, "Scientist Theorized Anthrax Mail Attack," *Baltimore Sun*, June 27, 2002.

spreading through the air and describes placing 2.5 grams of Bacillus globgii, used to simulate anthrax, in an envelope. Almost the same amount of anthrax was used in each of the letters in the Amerithrax attacks.

Despite this history, the FBI waited until June 25, 2002 to search the Detrick Plaza apartment of the biowarfare researcher, removing property from it while declaring that Dr. Hatfill is not a suspect. Dr. Hatfill is just one of about 30 US-based biowarfare experts the FBI is investigating, and one of more than two dozen whose homes have been searched with their owners' permission. Yet the search of Dr. Hatfills apartment was conducted with much more publicity than any of the others. Is Dr. Hatfill a potential patsy, is the FBI merely negligent in its investigation, or is it covering for Dr. Hatfill? According to a microbiologist interviewed by reporters for the *Hartford Courant*, the search was, "...strictly for show—a bone tossed to Congress and the media— or they want to put pressure on him by starting a public investigation to stimulate the stalled non-public investigation."[1] Does Dr. Hatfill know secrets which could come out in a public trial, secrets which, for whatever reason, the government does not wish disclosed?

Given the large amount of evidence, and the very small pool of potential suspects, it is bewildering why the FBI has not discovered more leads, or made a single arrest in the Amerithrax

---

[1] Dave Altimari, Jack Dolan, and David Lightman, "The Case of Dr. Hatfill: Suspect Or Pawn," *Hartford Courant*, June 27, 2002.

investigation. In contrast with the thousands of innocent Arabs and Muslims detained, often without legal council or opportunity for bail, since September 11, there has been only one detention regarding the anthrax letters—that of Clayton Lee Wagner, a fugitive before the attacks, who was convicted on admitted hoaxes, but had no knowledge of the actual attacks.

Almost immediately after the skyjackings, in fact within hours, American authorities named Osama bin Laden as the prime suspect. The names and photographs of the nineteen skyjackers were quickly released to the public, along with detailed information concerning their movements over the last few years leading up to the attack, demonstrating their links to bin Laden and al-Qaeda. In light of the years of close surveillance of al-Qaeda and foreknowledge of a domestic terror attack from bin Laden's organization, this is not surprising. Given the premeditated war against Afghanistan, planned for years in advance, it is not surprising that the White House would immediately make its case to the American people and allied governments around the world that al-Qaeda and its sponsors in Afghanistan, the Taliban, were responsible and needed to be punished. Yet, given the far smaller pool of suspects in the Amerithrax investigation, it is surprising that the FBI has not produced a suspect in these attacks. Reports on the progress of this investigation have dropped off the American media horizon, and must in many cases be followed in the foreign press, even though it is likely that the perpetrator is an American citizen.

As mentioned above, the technical expertise needed to mount the attack and the physical evidence obtained from it, points to a small pool of potential suspects. Yet, as the *Baltimore Sun* reported on December 9, 2001, "Two months after the FBI mobilized hundreds of agents to investigate the anthrax attacks, the bureau still has not interviewed the only Americans with experience producing anthrax for use as a weapon: aging veterans of the US biological warfare program based at Fort Detrick."

The Amerithrax terror incident and the subsequent FBI handling of the investigation raise a number of troubling questions, questions that have implications regarding all of the terror events in the autumn of 2001 and government activities through the time of this writing in 2002.

Who else but people connected to the state could have developed and weaponized the anthrax used in these attacks? Very few individuals or organizations in the world possess the knowledge or facilities necessary for the production of such high grade, concentrated, hardy, and dispersible anthrax spores. All of the biological clues available indicate the anthrax used was developed, if not in fact manufactured, at the US Army Medical Research Institute for Infectious Diseases at Fort Detrick, Maryland.

Who else but people connected to the state could have mailed the anthrax letters, and the subsequent hoaxes, at the end of September and beginning of October 2001? As difficult as the production of such highly refined, unmilled, weapons grade bacteria is, even handling the deadly spores is in and of itself a dangerous proposition. Consider that the entire Senate and House office buildings were found to be contaminated by a few grams of the pathogen, and that a boy walking through the NBC studios contracted anthrax poisoning. Whoever handled the bacteria had most likely been vaccinated against the bacteria. Records of anthrax vaccinations are carefully kept and only a relatively few people in the world have received the experimental vaccine.

Why would the assailant use an Islamic cover? In the letters mailed to Senators Daschle and Leahy and NBC News anchor Tom Brokaw, the date "09-11-01" and the words, "Death To America," "Death To Israel," and "Allah Is Great" were rendered in an obviously altered block script. Additionally, there was the accusatory letter naming a scientist at USAMRIID with an Mid-Eastern name as a terrorist. Although it is obvious why the attacker might want to deflect attention from the true origin of the attacks, it still leads to other questions. The preparation of the anthrax used would have taken far longer than the seven days between the skyjackings and the anthrax attacks. Was the assailant waiting for an opportunity to deploy the deadly bug? Or did the assailant have foreknowledge of the September 11 disaster?

Why were the particular targets picked? Why was the White House not attacked and why did White House staff begin taking Cipro right after 9-11? Why were senators more closely identified

167

with foreign policy not attacked, such as Senator Jesse Helms of South Carolina? Or prominent Jewish senators closely identified with Israel, such as former vice-presidential candidate Joseph Lieberman of Connecticut? The assailant chose the leader of the Democratic opposition and the chairman of the Senate Judiciary Committee, a committee solely concerned with domestic issues, for obvious political reasons.

The anthrax attacks were clearly timed to coincide with the skyjackings of September 11, yet the amount of time needed to prepare such weapons grade pathogens would have been far longer than the seven days between the hijackings and the mailing of the anthrax letters. The letters were sent to the Senators during the brief debate around the Patriot Act, and ceased shortly after the act was signed into law. The poison letters were meant to influence the senators and the American public into accepting an increase in police power.

Where is the investigation into the Amerithrax case? The attackers left many clues, both biological and behavioral, yet the FBI has been very slow to follow even the most obvious of leads and all too ready to present a lone wolf profile, akin to Lee Harvey Oswald and James Earl Ray, rather than consider this a group operation. Recent revelations have shown that leads uncovered by agents in the field have been squashed by superiors in Washington, DC. Has the Amerithrax investigation been stalled by high-level FBI officials? If so, why?

The Amerithrax case leaves us with more questions than any other in this troublesome period. We suggest that the state either turned a blind eye or was directly involved in the attack and its cover-up. The timing of the attack, so close to 9-11 and contemporaneous with debate on Patriot Act, indicates the strategy of tension was in play by ruthless politicians who will do anything to get their way. We must continue to ask pointed questions until we receive honest answers, lest the lack of explanation be its own reply.

III.

Epilogue

"Universal history is the tribunal of the world."
August von Cieszkowski, *Prolegomena to Historiosophy*

We are not the first to use the title Shadow Government as careful readers of our notes realize,[1] and we do so, 1) in the sense that this government casts gloom far beyond Washington and its bunkers in Greenbrier, West Virginia, whence it advances the war on terrorism; and 2) in the sense that this is a secretive state that went underground without telling Congress and that continues to somehow obscure the malice in its actions. The post-9-11 executive orders signed along with a declaration of a state of emergency remind us of continuity of government planning by Oliver North that called for martial law and suspension of the Constitution.

Autonomedia has compiled an indicative list of these executive orders[2] that Bush signed after invoking the National Emergencies Act in September 2001. These orders are not subject to congressional review and allow the government wide-

---

[1] Cf., chapter I, section 6, a reference to Iran-Contra.
[2] autonomedia.org, info exchange; the official listing is at the National Archives website.

ranging power to take over all modes of transport (10990), to seize and control the media (10995), control all energy (10997), to take over food resources (10998), register all people (11002), and mobilize citizens into work brigades (11000). Forgive us for invoking Draco—author of the notoriously severe first Athenian law code, published in 621 BC[1]—and the overused term *draconian* to describe these executive orders. How else, with universal history in mind, could we describe orders that allow the government to relocate communities and designate areas to be abandoned (11004), or control wages, salaries, credit, and flow of money (11921)?

In July 2002, Bush signed the Public Health Security and Bioterrorism Act of 2002 and it became public law. Legislation on Model Emergency Health Preparedness (MEHPA), which was authored in Washington, is being promulgated in state assemblies. The bioterrorism law's $4.6 billion price tag, which is be so beneficial to the pharmaceutical industry because of vaccine research and development, was justified by the Amerithrax attacks. MEHPA gives states the right to arrest people who refuse treatment of drugs, including those that have not been tested on humans.

We have closely observed the process by which the president declared and then initiated legislation for his Department of Homeland Security (DHS) in summer 2002. We

---

[1] Aristotle, *The Athenian Constitution* (London, 1984).

follow with a sense of foreboding the debate between the White House and congressional authorizers and appropriators on what form this department will take. It may be composed of elements from many, we hear twenty-two, other departments. While this is going on, we keep in mind how Homeland Security will have unprecedented powers, exemptions from current law, such as the Freedom of Information Act. We simultaneously consider how DHS might abuse aspects of the USA Patriot Act[1] in the new institution's ballyhooed goal of "connecting the dots" and we think of the shadows cast by vultures as they swoop on prey.

Meanwhile, we applaud reports of citizens in New England meeting to contest the Patriot Act because nothing in current law will be able to stop this new department, or others, from conducting surveillance without warrants and using the information in a criminal trial. The CIA, which is responsible for millions of deaths in its covert operations, can now operate domestically. The Justice Department has been eavesdropping on attorney-client conversations without court permission and making secret deportations; the FBI is considering using Israeli interrogation methods on detainees, such as drugging and pressure tactics.[2]

On Capitol Hill, a few senators have criticized the CIA and FBI but they do so in a way that takes these agencies admissions of repeated failures at face value without considering that once

---

[1] Cf., chapter I, section 11.
[2] Suzanne Crowell, "Bush and Ashcroft Unleashed," *Democratic Left*, Spring 2002, 6.

back in their bureaucracies, as their budgets and powers increase as a result of potentially false confessions, these paramilitary monsters snarl with delight over what was quite successful from their perspective. Virtually every intelligence failure in recent US history has been blamed on "noncoordination"?[1] In his conclusion to his book on FBI-CIA strife, Mark Riebling says that "If our pragmatism suggests that the best remedy for the FBI-CIA war is probably some sort of superagency, our idealism," opposed to a police state, "guarantees that no such final solution will ever be tried."

Riebling and other experts should understand that these paramilitary agents relish going back to the days of red squads and Cointelpro to again harass citizens at will.[2] What does it say about our form of government when the most democratic forces in civilian society are subject to infiltrators and provocateurs, disinformation and misdirection? How does the US government rule when it uses the defensive terror described in our state-terror thesis? It rules by terror.

We understand that the state, *stato* for Machiavelli, in *The Prince* is a means of exploitation, a way to do something to someone else, a way to acquire advantage. Acquisition becomes the *raison d'état* and moral restraints loosen.[3] In the case of empire,

---

[1] Mark Riebling, *Wedge* (New York, 1994), 495.
[2] Frank Donner, *Protectors of Privilege* (Berkeley, 1990); Ward Churchill and Jim Vander Wall, *Conitelpro Papers* (Boston, 1990).
[3] Harvey Mansfield, *Machiavelli's Virtue* (Chicago, 1966), 290–1.

especially for Hobbes, the state becomes a predatory beast, a Leviathan bent on conquest.

Hobbes reminds us that Romans thought of themselves as having *pacified* other provinces when people expressly or tacitly submitted to the government.[1] The Goths would not be pacified and refused to pay subsidies to Roman temples, which were confiscated. Followers of Roman religion were massacred in some cities of the empire; slaves opened the city gates for Alaric as he marched on Rome on August 24, 410. The Eternal City fell into the hands of barbarians and the empire crumbled for decades until it ceased to exist.

How long will the American Empire last? As was said in the twentieth century of the French Revolution, it's too early to tell. We are not prophets, but we understand the dialectical logic in blowback, a term that denotes the unforeseen and disastrous domestic consequences of a misguided foreign operation. Chalmers Johnson informs us that the term *blowback* was first used in March 1954 to describe the coup operation against Mohammed Mossadegh in Iran.[2] The CIA-imposed Shah government's repression engendered the Iranian revolution and US hostage crisis.

The classic example for us, however, is given by Christopher Simpson in *Blowback*. Those of us who despise fascists recall that the United States recruited Nazi spy chief

---

[1]   Thomas Hobbes, *Leviathan* (New York, 1985), 720.
[2]   Chalmers Johnson, "Blowback," *Nation*, October 15, 2001, 13.

Reinhard Gehlen; his exaggerated threat of an attack from the Soviet Union found its way into military appropriations bills in the post-war period, which dumped "millions of dollars into a variety of covert operations and intelligence programs, including the newly born CIA and its chief client, the Gehlen Organization."[1]

Blowback in the case of Afghanistan is seen in the way the United States created a training ground for the jihadists now lurking in our midst. US support for the mujahideen in the liberation of Afghanistan tens of thousands of Muslim fighters were armed and trained by the United States, Saudi Arabia, and Pakistan. Mujahideen mercenaries, members of al-Qaeda, were recruited, with US and NATO complicity, to fight with the drug-dealing Kosovo Liberation Army (KLA), which was once equated in the Senate with "American values."[2] The projection of US power through allies like this values expediency and power. This global power game turns our military and paramilitary institutions into our enemies when blowback strikes at home in covert operations such as 9-11 and the Amerithrax attacks.

The truth is that the United States and Saudi Arabia invested $6 billion in Islamic jihad, using Pakistan's Inter-Services

---

[1] Christopher Simpson, *Blowback* (New York, 1988), 59-64; idem, *The Splendid Blond Beast* (New York, 1993), 53-7, on early and sustained U.S. commercial ties with, and investment in, Hitler's major supporters in German manufacturing and banking sectors.

[2] Michel Chossudovsky, "Osamagate, the Whole Story," *True Democracy*, October 9, 2001, 5; although not an exhaustive study, the articles collected in Paul Virilio's *Stratégie de la deception* (Paris,.1999) point out NATO's tactics in Kosovo.

Intelligence for cover. It is now fairly well-known that after the Soviet withdrawal, Afghanistan became a university for jihad, a school for terrorists and assassins, but prior to 9-11, say, back in the late seventies and early eighties, who knew the United States was spawning Islamic terrorists? Only cynical people in Washington with hatred for Moscow knew because they were the ones who secretly aimed hatred at Kabul. This same hate was eventually redirected against New York and Washington on Black Tuesday.

Zbigniew Brzezinski concedes to the French press that on July 3, 1979, President Carter authorized aid to anti-Soviet forces in Afghanistan to induce the Russians to intervene, which they did five months later. The idea was to award the Soviets their Vietnam regardless of the consequences of creating "some stirred-up Moslems."[1] We agree with those who consider the Afghan war, not so much the threat of Star Wars, to have shaken the foundations and precipitated the collapse of empire. For Russia, the war was worse than our Vietnam.

Under Reagan, the war against the pro-Soviet Afghan regime of Barak Karmal escalated. Former campaign director, then CIA Director, William Casey made it his personal mission to spread subversive propaganda throughout the region by having the CIA distribute Korans, books on Soviet atrocities, and books on local nationalism. We completely missed the story, to cite

---

[1] Zbigniew Brzezinski, interview in *Le Nouvel observateur*, January 15, 1998, 76.

another example of US propaganda tactics involving hate, about the amazingly violent jihadist school textbooks, created and edited at the University of Nebraska. The United States supplied these books to Afghanistan, but the story only emerged after the attacks. Voice of America, moreover, supposedly had a Pashtun broadcaster known as Kandahar Rose to her colleagues because of her pro-Taliban slant.

The connections go even deeper. Some of the training camps we have bombed were built by the United States and were used by the CIA to train mujaheddin rebels in secret communications and use of timing devices for "C-4 plastic explosives for urban sabotage," among other techniques.[1] By 1987, the United States was sending 65,000 tons of arms supplies to the mujaheddin via their Pakistani advisors. This was a major operation, based on tried if untrue techniques, spreading virulent propaganda and then following it up with violence.

Once again, this time in *Science of Coercion*, Christopher Simpson shows what the world has been up against since the Second World War. This from the US Army's Joint Strategic Plans Committee, August 2, 1948:

Psychological warfare employs all moral and physical means, other than orthodox military operations, which tend to:

a. destroy the will and the ability of the enemy to fight;

---

[1] Steve Coll, "Anatomy of a Victory: CIA's Covert Afghan War," *Washington Post*, July 19, 1992; Tim Weiner, "Afghan Taliban Camps Were Built by NATO," *New York Times*, August 24, 1998.

b. deprive him of the support of his allies and neutrals;

c. increase in our own troops and allies the will to victory.

Psychological warfare employs any weapon to influence the mind of the enemy. The weapons are psychological only in the effect they produce and not because of the nature of the weapons themselves. In this light, overt (white), covert (black), and gray propaganda; subversion; sabotage; special operations; guerrilla warfare; espionage' political, cultural, economic, and racial pressures are all effective weapons. They are effective because they produce dissension, distrust, fear and hopelessness in the minds of the enemy, not because they originate in the psyche of propaganda or psychological warfare agencies.

Simpson points out that the reference to special operations denoted, among other things, assassination, and that these psychological warfare operations were directed against the American population, as were biological warfare experiments (Cf. Timeline). We highly recommend Simpson's book and its bibliographic essay for those who want to know how it would dawn on people to engineer these campaigns to create tension to justify war and repression. Blowback and a willingness to use a fatal expression of it for these sinister ends, which only spread more hatred, explain 9-11 and Amerithrax attacks—as if so many wrongs could possibly make it right. The spin is so hard that the White House spokesman actually asked, in an accusing way, about Democrats: If they knew about 9-11 in advance, why didn't they do something?[1]

---

[1] n.a., "Rebuke From Feinstein," *San Francisco Chronicle–SFGate.com*, May 18, 2002.

Bush had the audacity to tell the U.N. General Assembly in November 2001, "We must speak the truth about terror. Let us never tolerate outrageous conspiracy theories concerning the attacks of September 11, malicious lies that attempt to shift the blame away from the terrorists themselves, away from the guilty." The president with questionable legitimacy may have to learn to tolerate conspiracy theories, other than the US government's conspiracy theories, because many of the victim's families are coming forth with wrongful death suits against him and against other members of his administration with the theory that you Let It Happen On Purpose (LIHOP). People know statesmen wanted to replay the Great Game, the nineteenth century Anglo-Russo diplomatic gamesmanship in Central Asia, what Ahmed Rashid in *Taliban* calls the New Great Game, and we suspect that 9-11 was a big move in that game.

Energy interests, over the years, have attained great influence over US foreign policy in the region, but had to contend with a more Russian-oriented policy under Clinton. Bush made it clear from the start that he would not defer to the Russians on much of anything and unilaterally abrogated or withdrew from treaties. We have found out, after the fact, that the war was planned and threatened against the Taliban. Why? Why wouldn't a war with the Taliban have been in large part for the sake of the US oil industry, particularly its Houston focal point? We think the political class and their industrial backers cashed in big chips on 9-11. These chips appear to have served inside stock speculators and as bait for the invasion of Afghanistan.

Any honest analysis would hold that statesmen acted on behalf of their class, more specifically, on behalf of the energy industry, members of which comprise so much of the current administration. "Bush has named at least 30 former energy industry executives, lobbyists and lawyers to influential jobs in the administration. Some of them have helped the government carry out major parts of the energy policy without waiting for Congressional action."[1] The *New York Times* quotes an industry executive as saying "The people running the United States government are from the energy industry. They understand it and they believe in energy supply."

These are people like Secretary of Commerce Donald Evans who worked for an oil and gas company, or White House Chief of Staff Andrew Card who was president of the American Automobile Manufacturers Association, or again Council on Environmental Quality Chief of Staff Philip Cooney who was a lawyer for the American Petroleum Institute. United States Trade Representative Robert Zoellick was on Enron's advisory council and a deputy secretary of interior who was a close ally of the mining lobby.

The notorious Thomas White, secretary of the army, is emblematic of the degree to which the energy industry dominates

---

[1] Don Van Natta, Jr., with Neela Banerjee, "Bush Policies Have Been Good to Energy Industry," *New York Times*, April 21, 2002, 24.

the government. From 1998 to 2001, White was vice-chairman of Enron Energy Services and, according to news accounts, personally misled analysts, salespeople, and investors in a Ponzi scheme that netted him millions of dollars. Enron was the energy company that went bust because of mismanagement and lost shareholders money. White violated his pledge to divest from Enron when he joined the Department of Defense and then divested right before the stock fell. White has admitted to having had previously undisclosed contacts with Enron while at his government position.

Government from behind the scenes, such as Senator Phil Gramm slipping a bill into the 2000 omnibus appropriations measure that exempted energy trading from regulation, becomes the rule. Gramm's wife Wendy was head of the Commodity Futures Trading Commission where she set policies that exempted financial instruments favored by Enron from federal regulation; she then quit the CFTC and became a director at Enron where she made scads of money. The public should know by now what Cheney, formerly of Halliburton, and Enron CEO Kenneth Lay spoke about in April 2001, beyond the three-page wish list of Enron recommendations, much of which, according to a congressional analysis, was adopted by Cheney's energy task force. Halliburton subsidiary Brown and Root, after all, helped build Houston's Enron Field.[1]

---

[1] Readers interested in Halliburton's drug connection should read Michael

Waxman asserts no company stood to gain as much by the task force proposals as Enron. What's more, we know that Cheney told the *Los Angeles Times*, the day after he met with his primary campaign contributor Lay, "Kenny-Boy" to Bush the Younger, in April 2001. Cheney told the paper that price caps were out of the question.

What will it take for Enron to become Bush's Teapot Dome, another scandal involving oil and greed. Perhaps it will require more evidence to surface, 1) showing 9-11 to have been a stratagem to manipulate markets—the SEC has so far not told the public who profited from the attacks; and 2) showing that the attacks were allowed to happen to provide a pretext to wage a war that would make it safe—a still dubious prospect—for a gas pipeline through Afghanistan to Enron's energy plant in India.

How powerful was Enron? It was a global empire, ranking seventh in the United States and sixteenth in the world in terms of size. Enron was the world's largest energy trader with its tentacles in many other sectors.[1] As successful as Enron was in Washington at obtaining its policy objectives, such as naming regulators and blocking moves to regulate offshore tax havens, it enjoyed success in Geneva, at the World Trade Organization, on liberalizing trade in financial services. This leads to privatization of basic services. Its goal was to own and exploit gas, oil, and water pipelines in far-flung points on the globe.

Ruppert, "The Bush-Cheney Drug Empire," *From the Wilderness*, October 24, 2000.
[1] John Nichols, "Enron's Global Crusade," *Nation*, March 4, 2002.

Enron's Dabhol power-plant project, which the World Bank said was not viable, spawned considerable local resistance. The energy company fought the movement by paying police who dragged activists out of their homes and beat them. Human Rights Watch called it "brutal human rights violations carried out on behalf of the state's and the company's interests." Enron spent $20 million on so-called educational gifts in India, apparently spending as lavishly on Maharashtra state officials as on those in the United States. How was it that as Enron was lauded as emblematic of globalization at home while causing scandal after scandal overseas? From cutthroat financial tactics applied to freshly deregulated markets to environmental and human rights abuses on a global scale, Enron represents the terrors of globalization come home to roost for the now empty-handed shareholders who financed these misdeeds for so many years. It was Enron, to mention another example, which instantly profited from Operation Desert Storm, which conveniently expanded Kuwaiti boundaries, by gaining the jacked-up contract through Bush family and former Bush administration officials, to rebuild a power plant in Shuaiba. Was Enron the intended beneficiary of the globalization of terror as it returned to origins in a spectacular way? Would it thereby get its pipeline and cover for its accounting shenanigans.

Who can understand this hairy knot called Black Tuesday? The loyal opposition waits its turn or colludes or works gently behind the scenes, as they do on Capitol Hill, for another merry go round session. Through circumstances of his or his masters' making, George Bush finds himself at a moment when he can be Cæsar who, despite his limitations, proceeded from conquest to conquest and wrote about himself in the third person as if he truly consummated his role more than anyone in history.[1]

All too often the stage of history is occupied by great men like Julius who engaged Egypt, Pontus, Africa, and Spain and became master of the Roman world. President Bush would have us rally around him like Cæsar, and the conquest of Afghanistan, as impressive as it was, is nothing compared with what Bush outlined in his West Point speech in the summer of 2002 that makes us wary Bush will march on Iraq and numerous other points on the axis of evil, without pretext so much as a presumed, what will likely be extralegal, preemption. First Iraq, hawks in the Defense Department strategize, then other corrupt Middle East regimes will fall, such as Saudi Arabia and Egypt. Never mind the possibility that other Arab nations will fight with Iraq.

The new strategic doctrine informs the world that the United States will take care of its security problems and simultaneously expand its dominance in every aspect of war, notably those used in the War on Terror against an evasive

---

[1] Cæsar, *The Civil War* (New York, 1967): "... Pothinus, the king's tutor and regent, who was in Cæsar's part of town, was sending messengers to Achillas urging him not to slacken in his efforts or lose heart. His intermediaries were betrayed and arrested, and Pothinus was put to death by Cæsar. These events were the beginning of the Alexandrian War."

nonstate enemy, but also including far-out plans for the weaponization of space. The global presence of the US military is expanding, and if the record is any indication, we will leave behind a place far worse than we found it.

Are US military interventions designed to stabilize other countries or to impose Washington's will? How does it help to bomb poor people, such as the Afghan wedding party in summer 2002? It saddens us to think of the depleted uranium from exploded US bombs spreading far and wide as dustlike particles, killing people with cancer for generations to come. As Tacitus remarked on conquest of Britain: "The Roman army created desolation and called it peace."

Bush seems willing to be judged in relation to bin Laden rather than for anything good he could accomplish. And compared to more attacks by al-Qaeda, anything Bush does seems justified or at least passable to citizens who crave security. Threats, arrests, warnings—they justify more enclosures by the state, such as retinal scanners and facial recognition technology that photograph more movements than we can remember. We could well find ourselves in a situation where such extensive security measures are taken—at the expense of human rights and to the benefit of the police, military, and intelligence agencies— right when we begin to doubt the evidence that justified these measures. Then it's too late. Some will have been duped, others maintain skepticism as long as they can, and still others are made to believe by force.

The jury of universal history, Hegel's total history, is still out on Bush the Younger, although he will always be considered not in relation to Cæsar, who more resembles Clinton, but to Napoleon because of Bush's pedigree in a particular semisecret society. We recall how much Napoleon Bonaparte inspired Hegel and Clausewitz to study war and how influential Hegel is with Yale's Skull and Bones. Yes, we're referring to the infamous Order of Skull and Bones that emanates from Yale and infiltrates the Council on Foreign Relation (CFR) while maintaining ties with another Anglo-American semisecret society, the Group, which was studied in detail by the late Anthony Sutton in *America's Secret Establishment*.[1]

If you doubt the power of secret societies, you might do well to research the power of Bones men since the inception of the Order in 1833. What a gruesome image it is, this world of ours being spun by black-hooded brothers. The Group, founded at Oxford University, rests on the more festive image of a round table, but its goals for Anglo-American world domination overlap with the Order's creation of a New World Order by means of such coercive measures as wars and revolutions. They like to pit sides against each other in a conflict of opposites whose outcome is assured once they come in to manage the situation.

It's Hegelian at its core in its crude application of negation. Wars, depressions, assassinations, theft—they use these acts to

---

[1] Antony C. Sutton, *America's Secret Establishment: Introduction to the Order of Skull & Bones* (Billings, 1986).

set events in motion that favor their class and personal interests. They are gangsters who profit both from turning the world into rubble and rebuilding it in the image of nightmares like Houston; men for whom Islamic terrorists are an convenient device to initiate change. The Black Tuesday attacks could be seen, with this logic, as a negation that is negated by war with Afghanistan, which may be regrettable, but is profitable, especially for the Carlyle Group where Bush the Elder holds court. As this dialectic may have been described to Bush the Younger, bad things will happen, so more bad things will happen, then everything will be wonderful for you and a flag-waving country.

We can find another use for Hegel's logic, to digress, with respect to 9-11. Every logical entity has three sides: abstract, dialectical, speculative.[1] The abstract stage of understanding 9-11 requires historical knowledge and anticipatory thinking to know how states have acted and likely will act in the future. The dialectical moment enables us to understand how states pass into their opposites, into the terrorists they should oppose. The speculative side involves apprehending the reason behind a unity of terms in opposition, such as *defensive attack*. Hegel glorified war between states as being in the ethical health of a people, a notion taken up by Nazis, and he glorified his beloved Prussian monarchy for maintaining order on the homeland front. The

---

[1]   G.W.F. Hegel, Science of Logic (New York, 1975), 113.

state was, for Hegel, the final form of the Spirit and only the return of history will prove him wrong.

Yale denies that Skull and Bones is a chapter of a German secret society, but evidence emerged when the Temple was raided in 1876—a card was found that clearly originated from the German Chapter. In conspiracy theory circles, people like to speculate on something called the Illuminati,[1] Adam Weishaupt's society that recruited students from Ingolstadt University. Skull and Bones infected the United States in 1833, at Yale, when future General William Russell brought it back with him from study in Germany, in 1833. This was only forty-eight years after the elector of Bavaria abolished the Illuminati sect. Weishaupt's disciples turned over to Russell what both the Illuminati and Skull and Bones refer to internally as the Order.

We were amazed and astounded to find out that the Union Banking Corporation of New York City helped finance the Nazi party more than any other overseas bank and six of its eight directors were either Nazis or members of the Order, members like Prescott S. Bush, patriarch of the Bush political clan. The Order shares with Nazis a fetish for occult rituals, like Supreme Court Justice Potter Stewart, dressed as a skeleton and howling at a Bones initiate who was reclining in a velvet-lined coffin. The initiate then has a bone with his name on it tossed into the bone heap before plunging naked into a mud pile with other initiates.

---

[1] Robert Shea and Robert Anton Wilson, *Illuminatus! Trilogy* (New York, 1975).

We find it macabre that the ex-head of the CIA with a Skull and Bones pedigree could become president of the United States by succeeding a president he, Bush the Elder, ushered into office with the covert operation known as October Surprise.[1] As a vice presidential candidate who was not in power, Bush apparently traveled to Paris, on October 19, 1980, or was otherwise involved with a team that negotiated with Iranians to keep American hostages in captivity until after Reagan assumed office, which is what happened—the hostages were released immediately after Reagan was inaugurated. What was the vice president's alibi? He claims, although this could not be verified, to have had brunch at a country club with the now deceased Justice Potter Stewart. President Bush the Elder was a Skull and Bones man who had Second World War-era fascists and vocal fascist sympathizers on his transition team.[2]

Bush the Younger came into office, as Greg Palast has shown,[3] through blatant election fraud on the part of his brother, governor of Florida. The crisis of legitimacy surrounding the most democratic aspect of our republic, voting, is magnified by the accounting and banking scandals that go to the core of the political economy. These scandals—from Enron to WorldCom, Harken to Halliburton, to Anderson and beyond—call the legitimacy of institutions of financial capital into question because

[1] Gary Sick, *October Surprise* (New York, 1991); Robert Parry, *October Surprise X-Files:Hidden Origins of the Reagan-Bush Era* (Arlington, 1996).
[2] Russ Bellant, *Old Nazis, the New Right, and the Republican Party* (Boston, 1991).
[3] Greg Palast, *The Best Democracy Money Can Buy* (London, 2002).

the same autocratic and secretive corporate form of governance, relying heavily on industrial espionage and covert tactics, has moved back into the White House.

Bush or those with sway over him used illegitimately obtained power, circumstances suggest, to orchestrate or allow the Black Tuesday attacks as a pretext to invade Afghanistan for economic, specifically energy, interests and to tighten the paramilitary grip on restless populations. We feel disgraced by these dirty tricksters who lack the majesty to occupy high office and who project such a rosy future *for* war.[1] They annul our civil liberties as they rule by terror, using threats of terror to take every advantage. May shadows be destroyed by the sun.

---

[1] Philippe Delmas, *Rosy Future of War* (New York, 1995).

Timeline

"Just as Fortune has steered almost all the affairs of the world in one direction and forced them to converge upon one and the same goal, so it is the historian's task to present to the reader under one synoptical view the process by which she has accomplished this general design."

Polybius, *Rise of the Roman Empire*

The following timeline comprises deceptive actions by institutions and individuals, states and statesmen, along with numerous contextual facts. The events span a century and three continents to demonstrate the use of stratagems and their consequences, which is often war. The terrorist attacks against the United States on September 11 likewise make us ask if the dice were loaded, if we were dealt cards from a stacked deck, if the neat box in which the executive branch statesmen placed the attacks had a false bottom.

These deceptive actions pertain not only to the individuals involved in the September 11 tragedy, but also to their institutions. We find that individuals disclose their malevolent motivations through deceptive behavior; the same is true for the motives of institutions that favor these practices. Just as individual memory and capabilities affect personal decisions, institutional memory and immense power account for the motives and behavior we find in states and statesmen. In the context of the military and the state, history shows that soldiers and statesmen repeat their roles as deceivers of the public when it comes to occurrences that that give rise to war, even to the extent of terrorizing fellow citizens.

February 15, 1898—The *USS Maine* sinks in a mysterious explosion in Cuban waters, killing 254 sailors and wounding 59 others. The ship was called to Havana harbor by ex-General Fitzhugh Lee, nephew of Confederate General Robert E. Lee, and at the time American consul to Cuba. The *Maine's* mission was purportedly to "protect American interests" but its sinking would become the pretext for the invasion of Cuba and the initiation of the Spanish-American War. The motive for this war was to extend American military and economic domination not only in the Caribbean, but also in the South Pacific through the Philippines. The first people to come to the rescue were sailors from the Spanish ship Alfonso XII, but the American press was quick to blame the Spanish. The flames of war were fanned by press giants William Randolph Hearst and Joseph Pulitzer. In a quote that would resonate throughout the history of the twentieth century, in reference to the blast, Hearst wired artist Frederick Remington, "You furnish the pictures, I'll furnish the war." Even after an extensive investigation by the US Navy, the cause of the explosion was never explained.

May 7, 1915—The British passenger liner Lusitania is directed to cross the Atlantic and break a German U-boat blockade despite repeated prior attacks and public warnings of unrestricted firing. The Admiralty in London calls off the luxurious flagship's escort and she sails into what a serious historian who specializes in British naval intelligence says was a trap designed to bring Washington into the war.

1925—Geneva Protocol prohibits use of chemical and biological weapons.

September 1, 1939—Hitler stages the seizure of the Gleiwitz Radio Station using Jews from concentration camps, dressed in Polish uniforms, as a pretext to declare war and invade Poland.

December 7, 1941—The Japanese Navy attacks the distant, but strategically important, American Naval base on Pearl Harbor. The Pacific fleet was crippled enough to justify entrance into the Second World War. Years later it became clear, through military

195

investigations, that plans for the attack were known in advance by military men and statesmen who intentionally allowed the Japanese to scupper older ships as a *casus belli* while the carrier fleet was at sea. After the scapegoating of soldiers and sailors in the field was shown to be a cover-up for senior officers in Washington and the executive, General George C. Marshall resigned for his role in the tragedy with admission that he served his superior more than his country.

1942—Roosevelt approves the establishment of biological warfare program that would fall under the auspices of the Army Chemical Warfare Service.

1943—Biological warfare agent development and testing begins at Camp, later Fort, Detrick in Maryland.

1940s-1950s—The United States, Canada, and Britain spray pathogens on the Bahamas. No records are kept of human death or illness caused by the spraying.

1955—The CIA uses Whooping Cough bacteria from Fort Detrick in field tests along Florida's Gulf Coast.

1946—Ronald Reagan becomes FBI informer number T-10, providing information on the activities on the activities of the Screen Actors Guild and others in Hollywood. People he named,

196

such as Larry Parks, Howard Da Silva, and Alexander Knox, were later called before the House Un-American Activities Committee and blacklisted in Hollywood.

Late 1940s—Operation Mockingbird entails the CIA recruiting American news organizations and journalists to become spies and disseminators of propaganda. The effort is headed by Frank Wisner, Allan Dulles, Richard Helms, and Philip Graham. Graham is publisher of *The Washington Post*. Eventually, the CIA's media assets will include ABC, NBC, CBS, *Time, Newsweek,* Associated Press, United Press International, Reuters, Hearst Newspapers, Scripps-Howard, Copley News Service, and more. By the CIA's own admission, at least 25 organizations and 400 journalists became CIA assets.

1950—Government conducts anthrax test from a Navy ship off the coast of San Francisco using "simulants."

November 4, 1952—The National Security Agency is established. The NSA, third major United States intelligence agency after the FBI and the CIA, would grow to be the largest and most secretive of the three. The lack of details in its massive budget and its lack of Congressional oversight would lead it to be nicknamed the "No Such Agency." We turn to Rhodri Jeffreys-Jones, *Cloak & Dollar*, 175, for the genesis, where he notes that the budget for its building was $35 million. NSA's contemporary budget is three times that of the CIA. Its main mission is electronic surveillance worldwide.

1953—Army conducts open air tests in Minneapolis and St. Louis using zinc cadmium sulfide.

1960s—Army releases various gases and hallucinogenic drugs in open-air tests in Utah and Maryland.

March 1962—Chairman of the Joint Chiefs of Staff General Lyman Lemnitzer proposes to Secretary of Defense Robert McNamara that a covert attack upon Americans "would provide justification for U.S. military intervention" in Cuba. Known as Operation Northwoods, the plan, which had the written approval of every member of the Joint Chiefs of Staff, included hijacking planes, sinking boats carrying Cuban refugees, terrorizing Miami and Washington, D.C., and blowing up an American ship in Cuban waters, to mention a few of the plan's many stratagems. In addition to Operation Northwoods, other plans for the invasion of Cuba raise the sinister specter of biological warfare attacks. The ironically named Marshall Plan envisioned the use of anthrax. General Lemnitzer's motives were well known—he believed that the country would be better off if the military took over. James Bamford, *Body of Secrets*, gives the best account we've found and we are indebted to him for reproducing important sections of the documents in support of the state-terror thesis.

August 2, 1964—Aggressive intelligence–gathering operations by the US Destroyer *Maddox,* together with coordinated attacks on North Vietnam by the South Vietnamese navy and the Laotian air force in the Tonkin Gulf, lead to the fabrication of an attack by North Vietnam, which was used as a pretext for war. On August 4 President Johnson appears on television to announce air strikes in retaliation for torpedo attacks that never occurred. Reports in the *Washington Post* and the *New York Times* regarding North Vietnamese aggression create the climate for the Gulf of Tonkin Resolution passed by Congress on August 7, which was essentially a declaration of war on North Vietnam. The war would claim more than 50,000 American and a million Vietnamese casualties.

1964-1968—US conducts nerve gas tests on Navy sailors in the Pacific with sarin, VX gas, and biological toxins.

February 1967—*Ramparts* magazine, a Catholic publication based on the West Coast and known for its opposition to the Vietnam War, reveals that the CIA had been in control of the international activities of the National Student Association. The *Ramparts* articles revealed that the CIA had not only financed compliant student leaders in pro-Vietnam War activities, but also arranged draft exemptions for them. Among the domestic organizations revealed to be infiltrated by the CIA were the National Education

Foundation representing 983,000 teachers, the American Newspaper Guild, the American Political Science Association, and the AFL-CIO.

1972—Biological Weapons Convention, signed by the United States, prohibits development, production, and stockpiling of biological weapons.

December 22, 1974—The *New York Times* publishes a report by investigative journalist Seymor Hersh that reveals illegal domestic activities of the CIA: "The CIA, directly violating its charter, conducted a massive illegal domestic intelligence operation during the Nixon administration against the anti-war movement and other dissident groups in the United States." It is worth noting that both Vice-President Cheney and Secretary of Defense Rumsfeld worked within the Nixon White House. Rumsfeld would later champion expanding intelligence spending during the first Bush administration, declaring it to be one of his key objectives.[1]

1975—Raymond Winall of the FBI reveals to the Senate Foreign Relations Committee that a member of Black September, the Palestinian group responsible for the deaths of eleven Israeli athletes at the 1972 Olympics in Munich, told the FBI he

---

[1] Rhodri Jeffreys-Jones, *Cloak & Dollar* (New Haven, 2002), 286.

obtained pilot training in the United States for future terrorist attacks.

September 1978—After intense negotiations overseen by President Jimmy Carter, Anwar al-Sadat and Menachem Begin sign the Camp David Peace Accords between Egypt and Israel.

Christmas Day, 1979—Soviet Red Army occupies Afghanistan.

1982—NIH relaxes guidelines on recombinant DNA research, allowing release of genetically altered organisms into the environment.

1983—Several NIH permits are issued for open-air experiments.

January 1984—The CIA mines the harbors of Nicaragua in violation of the December 1982 Boland Amendment that prohibited the CIA from arming the Contra rebels. This act of state terrorism led to a conviction in the International Court at The Hague, Netherlands. To this day, the United States stands practically alone in its opposition to the creation of a permanent International War Crimes Tribunal because of charges against its statesmen.

October 1984—The CIA is given partial exemption from the Freedom of Information Act (FOIA), which gives American citizens the right to request copies of government documents.

October 1984—It is revealed that John Kirkpatrick, a contract CIA agent, had written a manual for the Nicaraguan Contras. Included in the manual were instructions on murder, including the assassination of allies or other sympathetic figures so as to place blame on opponents in false-flag operations.

January 1986—Creation of the joint CIA-FBI Counterterrorism Center to catch Soviet double agents.

September 29, 1988—The United States Army signs the first contract in its history to buy large quantities of anthrax vaccine. The vaccine is considered experimental and soldiers are required to sign release forms for it to be administered.

September 29, 1988—11 strains of biological warfare agents, including 4 types of anthrax, are sent from the American Type Culture Collection company in Maryland to the Iraqi Ministry of Trade's Technical and Scientific Materials Import Division. One of these strains, number 11966, was developed in 1951 at Fort Detrick as part of the United States Army's biological warfare program.

February 23, 1989—The United States Department of Commerce bans the sale of anthrax and dozens of other pathogens with biological warfare potential to Iraq, Iran, Libya, and Syria.

August 2, 1990—Iraq invades Kuwait.

September 11, 1990—President George H.W. Bush delivers an historic address before a joint session of Congress, heralding war with Iraq.

November 1991—Future Oklahoma City conspirator Terry Nichols meets with Abu Sayyaf members Edwin Angeles, Abdul Hakim Murad, Wali-Khan, and Ramsey Yousef in Davao City, Philippines.

December 24, 1992—President George H.W. Bush pardons six high ranking former officials in connection with the Iran-Contra scandal shortly before leaving office.

December 29, 1992—Al-Qaeda terrorists bomb a hotel in Aden, Sudan that houses American troops, killing two Austrian tourists.

February 26, 1993—The World Trade Center in Manhattan is attacked by an explosives-loaded van parked in the basement garage. The attack kills five and wounds hundreds. Evidence uncovered during the trial of the alleged bombers and in tapes

203

made by the FBI's informant shows that the agency had prior knowledge of the attack and did not move to prevent it.

June 1994—A report commissioned by the Pentagon concludes that religious terrorists could hijack jets and crash them into the Pentagon or White House.

December 24, 1994—Algerians skyjack an Air France airliner and threaten to crash it into the Eiffel Tower. They are apprehended in Marseille.

January 1995—Police in the Philippines discover an Islamist terrorist bomb factory. An arrested suspect, Abdul Hakin Murad, reveals Ramsey Yousef's Manila plot, code named Bojinka, which means "loud bang" in Serbo-Croatian, to bomb eleven US planes flying from Asia in a single day. A variation on the plan called for hijacking an airplane and crashing it into the CIA. A second plane would crash into the Pentagon or World Trade Center. Murad told police about his pilot training in the United States and the files were passed to the FBI and CIA. Future Oklahoma City bombing conspirator Terry Nichols who is in the Philippines at the time, breaks his excursion ticket and books a one-way ticket back to the United States.

February 1995—Ramsey Yousef is arrested in Pakistan in connection with the World Trade Center bombing and later extradited to the United States, where he was tried and convicted. Authorities link him to Osama bin Laden.

April 19, 1995—Explosions annihilate one-third of the Alfred P. Murrah Federal Building in Oklahoma City Oklahoma—killing 169 people, including nineteen children – purportedly caused entirely by a truck bomb parked outside. Tim McVeigh would be arrested ninety minutes later for having a loose license plate and going eighty miles per hour. Associated Press reported that later that day, around 11:00 am, an emergency broadcast for rescue workers to evacuate the building because of "possible explosives planted in the building." CNN also reported the broadcast. KWTW-TV reported the Oklahoma Bomb Squad's disposal unit backed its trailer into the scene. Rescue workers were forced to wait for the removal of bombs before going after survivors. KFOR-TV reported that the "FBI has confirmed there is another bomb in the federal building." Investigator Phil O'Halloran quotes the head of the Oklahoma City Police Department, Bill Martin, stating that containers of mercury fulminate were found in the building. KPOC-TV interviewed assistant Oklahoma City fire chief John Hanson, who said they "found two undetonated bombs in the building as well as one rocket launcher in the building." A terrorism expert, Dr. Randall Heather, reportedly told Channel 4, "We have both of the bombs that were defused at the site and are being taken apart. We will be able to find out how they were made, and possibly who made them. These bombs are very sophisticated high explosives with maybe a little fertilizer damped around them." An all points bulletin would go out for a Chevrolet pickup occupied by two Middle Eastern men.[1]

August 1995—Osama bin Laden calls for guerilla war against American troops stationed in Saudi Arabia.

November 13, 1995—Five Americans and two Indians are killed in Riyadh. Bin Laden allegedly facilitated the attack.

1996-1998—National Security Agency monitors hundreds of phone calls from Osama bin Laden and key associates to people in London, Iran, Saudi Arabia, Pakistan, and Sudan via the Inmarsat communications satellite above the Indian Ocean. The agency knew the scope of the al-Queda organization, the makeup of its top leadership, and many of their activities, such as whom they contacted.[2]

April 20, 1996—President Clinton signs Anti-Terrorism Act into law.

May 1996—Under US pressure, Sudan expels Osama bin Laden; he moves to Afghanistan.

---

[1] Jim Keith, OKBOMB! *Conspiracy and Cover-up* (Lilburn, 1997) 14-17.
[2] James Bamford, *Washington Post*, June 2, 2002.

June 25, 1996—In an attack linked to bin Laden, Khobar Towers military complex in Saudi Arabia is bombed, killing 19 US servicemen.

August 23, 1996—Bin Laden issues his first declaration of jihad against Americans, using a telephone monitored by NSA agents.

September 1996—Taliban captures Jalalabad and Kabul.

October 1997—Kofi Annan creates the Group of Concerned Countries at the UN. The so-called Six Plus Two consist of the six countries bordering Afghanistan plus Russia and the United States.

November 1997—Taliban delegation headed by Mullah Mohammed Ghaus arrives in Houston to meet with executives from Unocal. They stay at a five-star hotel, visit the zoo, supermarkets, and the NASA Space Center.

December 1997—The Pentagon announces that it will vaccinate 2.4 million soldiers and reservists against anthrax.

December 4, 1997—Taliban delegation enters into negotiations over a proposed oil pipeline through Afghanistan. The negotiations will ultimately fail, allegedly because the Taliban wanted too much money.

207

1998—According to the *Philadelphia Inquirer*, May 26, 2002, in 1998, "the FBI learned that a bin Laden associate, Ihab Ali Nawawi, then a cabdriver in Orlando, Fla., had received training at the Airman Flight School in Norman, Okla. The FBI opened an investigation of the school. Nawawi was taken into custody, where he remains today, although he has not been charged."

February 23, 1998—Bin Laden issues fatwa for killing US civilians and military personnel worldwide.

August 7, 1998—Al-Qaeda bombs US embassies in Kenya and Tanzania, killing 220.

August 1998—Washington declares Osama bin Laden its "Most Wanted" fugitive.

August 20, 1998—US attacks Afghanistan with Tomahawk cruise missiles in retaliation for the August 7 embassy attacks.

November 1998—Justice Dept. hands down 238 count indictment against Osama bin Laden; $5 million reward offered for his capture.

June 7, 1999—The FBI places Osama bin Laden on its *Ten Most Wanted* list.

September 1999—A report for the CIA concludes that "Suicide bombers belonging to al-Qaeda's Martyrdom Battalion could crash-land an aircraft packed with high explosives…into the Pentagon, the headquarters of the Central Intelligence Agency, or the White House."

December 1999—The Millenium plot to bomb Los Angeles airport is discovered with the arrest of Ahmed Ressam, who is linked to al-Qaeda.

December 1999—A group of al-Qaeda terrorists, armed with knives, skyjack an Indian airliner and fly to Kandahar, Afghanistan. They cut the throat of a passenger and leave him to die.

January 6, 2000—flight 77 hijacker Khalid al-Midhar attends a meeting in Kuala Lumpur, Malaysia including al-Qaeda members. The CIA monitors the meeting, photographing the participants. It was first reported that the CIA did not immediately notify the FBI or INS. when al-Midhar and fellow skyjacker Nawaf al-Hamzi, also identified as a participant in the meeting, flew from Kuala Lumpur to the United States. It now appears that the CIA did inform the FBI on January 6, however, the Department of State was not notified by the CIA and in June 2001 granted al-Midhar a new visa in Saudi Arabia, a visa that allowed him to return to the United States. The CIA would again alert the FBI about the two eventual skyjackers in late August 2001. On June 2, 2002, it was disclosed that, in a classified chronology submitted to Congress, the CIA revealed it knew Khalid al-Midhar was linked to a suspect in the bombing of the Navy Destroyer *Cole*, but did not inform the FBI.

October 2000—US Navy destroyer *Cole* is bombed by al-Qaeda operatives.

December 2000—The CIA discovers that Khalid al-Midhar was associated with a Cole-bombing suspect. The CIA again failed to notify the FBI of this link to al-Qaeda.

December 24, 2000—German SWAT teams storm two apartments in Frankfurt. They had been tipped off to a plot planning an attack on the annual Christmas Fair in Strasbourg. The raid results in the arrests of five Algerian men who were apparently members of a bomb assembly team.

Late December 2000—Ahmed Ressam is arrested in what would turn out to be a plot to bomb the Los Angeles International Airport. A link to al-Qaeda is established.

March 15, 2001—British based Jane's International Security reports that the Bush administration was working with Iran,

India, and Russia in a united front against the Taliban. India would supply the Northern Alliance with intelligence and materiel while Russia and India both provide bases for deployment. India, Russia, and Iran would handle aid on the ground while the United States would cover intelligence support.

March 22, 2001—Federal Aviation Administration security officials warn airlines and airports of "the possibility that one or more terrorist groups affiliated with bin Laden" might carry out an attack on a US airline.

May 1, 2001—Louis Freeh resigns as director of the FBI; Thomas Pickard serves as acting director.

May 17, 2001—Secretary of State Colin Powell announces the grant of $43 million in US aid to the Taliban government in Afghanistan, ostensibly for their efforts at the eradication of opium poppy cultivation.

May 23, 2001—The White House announces the appointment of Zalmay Khalilzad to a position on the National Security Council as special assistant to the president and senior director for Gulf, Southwest Asia and other regional issues. Khalilzad is a former official in the Reagan and the first Bush administrations. After leaving the government, he went to work for Unocal.

June 21, 2001—In an interview with an Arab journalist, Osama bin Laden warns of a major terrorist attack on American targets.

June 22-July 31, 2001—The FAA issues four information circulars to the commercial airline industry warning of possible terrorist attacks. An Information Circular, or IC as they're called, is a memorandum issued by the FAA to commercial aviation companies regarding potential security threats or other warnings. No specific response is required from airlines. A Security Directive, or SD, is a memorandum issued by the FAA to commercial airlines regarding potential security threats requiring immediate response from the airlines, often for a specific duration of time.

June 23, 2001—United States Department of Justice indicts thirteen Saudis and one Lebanese for the June 25, 1996 attack on the Khobar Towers military base in Saudi Arabia that killed nineteen US servicemen. In announcing the indictments, Attorney General John Ashcroft states that "Americans are a high-priority target for terrorists."

June 26, 2001—CIA sources report there is a spike in intelligence reports about possible terrorist strikes against American targets.

June 28, 2001—CIA Director George Tenet warns national security advisor Condoleeza Rice that it is "highly likely" that a "significant al-Qaeda attack" will occur "in the near future."

July 2001—US and Russian officials meet with counterparts in India and Pakistan about plans for a military action against the Taliban in October 2001. An Indian official said that his country and Iran would facilitate the action while the United States and Russia would combat the Taliban with the help of Tajikistan and Uzbekistan. India foreign secretary Chokila Iyer met with the Indo-Russian joint working group on Afghanistan in Moscow, and the chief of the Russian Federal Security Bureau, Nicolai Patroshev, visited Tehran. According to the British Broadcasting Company[1] Pakistani Foreign Secretary Niaz Naik said he was told by senior American officials that military action against the Taliban would take place by the middle of October.

July 2001—CIA official meets with Osama bin Laden and Ayman al-Zawahari at the American Hospital in Dubai. As reported by French daily newspaper *Le Figaro*, which is owned by the Washington-based Carlyle Group, and by Radio France International, bin Laden arrived in Dubai on July 4 from Quetta Pakistan for treatments for his seriously infected kidneys, accompanied by his close associate al-Zawahari, considered by

---

[1] George Arney "US 'planned attack on Taliban' the wider objective was to oust the Taliban," Sept. 18 2001.

many to be the brains behind al-Qaeda. During the stay, the local CIA representative was seen going into bin Laden's room and, according to *Le Figaro*, the CIA man boasted to friends of having visited the Saudi-born millionaire. On July 15, when bin Laden left the hospital, the CIA man returned to headquarters in Langley. The CIA denies this happened.

July 2001—United States withdraws from the Geneva Biological Weapons Convention over the issue of inspections.

July 2, 2001—The FBI issues a warning of possible attacks from al-Qaeda. The warning discusses the possibility of strikes both overseas and in the United States.

July 4, 2001—Flight 77 hijacker Khalid Almidhar reenters the United States.

July 5, 2001—President George W. Bush asks Codoleeza Rice to investigate what measures intelligence agencies are taking in response to reported threats of imminent attack from al-Qaeda.

July 5, 2001—At a White House meeting, counterterrorism officials warn the FBI, FAA, and INS that a terrorist attack on the United States is imminent.

July 10, 2001—FBI agent Kenneth Williams, a 41-year-old counterterrorism agent in the Phoenix office, sends a memo to headquarters in Washington regarding the large number of suspected Islamic terrorists signing up to take flight training courses. Students had links to the radical London based leader Sheikh Omar Bakri. Some of the suspects at the local Embry-Riddle Aeronautical University had been asking a lot of questions about airport security. The memo proposed monitoring civil aviation schools around the country. The FBI did nothing.

July 26, 2001—CBS News reports that Attorney General John Ashcroft, because of a potential threat assessment, leased a private plane instead of flying commercial airlines like other cabinet members.

August 2, 2001—State Department Asian Affairs specialist Christina Rocca meets Taliban ambassador in Islamabad, allegedly delivering a military threat.

August 2001—"In August and early September close associates of bin Laden were warned to return to Afghanistan from other parts of the world by 10 September," Britain says in its "Responsibility for the Terrorist Atrocities in the United States, 11 September 2001." The remarkable document states that "Immediately prior to 11 September some known associates of bin Laden were naming the date for action as on or around 11 September."

215

August 2001—Morrocan undercover agent Hassan Dabou, who has infiltrated al-Qaeda in Afghanistan, is taken off his assignment that brings him close to bin Laden, and sent to the United States.

August 2001—Actor James Woods, according to an article by Seymour Hersh, says that on a domestic flight cross-country, he expressed his concerns to the flight crew about the possibility of a hijacking by four suspicious looking well-dressed Middle Eastern passengers. "The guys were in synch- dressed alike. They didn't have a drink and were not talking to the stewardess. None of them had a carry-on or a newspaper. Nothing." The flight attendant stated that she would file a report about the suspicious passengers.

August 6, 2001—At his ranch in Crawford, Texas, President Bush receives his security briefing, the Presidential Daily Brief, or PDB, from the CIA. The one-and-a-half page document, titled "Bin Laden Determined to Strike in U.S.," was an analytic report on al-Qaeda. The report claims hijackings by al-Qaeda are likely to happen within the United States.

August 15, 2001—Officials at the Pan Am International Flight Academy in Eagan Minnesota, a suburb of Minneapolis, report to the FBI that Zacorias Moussaoui has aroused their suspicions. He had inquired about flight lessons, specifying that he wished to learn to fly a Boeing 747, but not to take-off or land. He paid the $6,300 fee in cash. He had no previous training in flying even small aircraft. After four to six calls to the FBI, the school finally got a response. A flight instructor warned the FBI that a 747 loaded with fuel could be used as bomb.

August 17, 2001—Zacorias Moussaoui, a French born man of Moroccan descent, is arrested on immigration charges. An agent warns that Moussaoui is planning to fly something into the World Trade Center. FBI agents request a FISA warrant to search his laptop computer. Headquarters deny this request. A later search of his computer would reveal information on piloting and crop dusting downloaded from the Internet, as well as a flight simulator program.

August 20, 2001—In a September 15 interview with MSNBC, Russian President Vladimir Putin says he instructed his intelligence bureau in August to warn the United States and its counterparts of likely attacks on airports and other targets.

August 23, 2001—flight 77 skyjacker Khalid Almidhar is put on the INS/FBI watch list seven weeks after he had reentered the United States, too late to be found.

August 26, 2001—French intelligence notifies FBI headquarters that Moussaoui is a suspected terrorist with ties to al-Qaeda. A special counterterrorism panel of the FBI and the CIA concludes he is not a threat, despite the French allegations and his refusal to answer questions. The now infamous Rowley memo reveals the lengths that headquarters went to find excuses to prevent her and her colleagues in the field from obtaining a search warrant. Moussaoui remains in INS detention, not to be transferred to the FBI until after September 11.

August 30, 2001—President Bush ends his month-long vacation at his ranch in Crawford, Texas, the longest Presidential vacation in three decades. He had spent 42% of his eight months in office either on the ranch, at Camp David, or at his family's compound in Maine, according to *The Washington Post.*

September 2001—President Bush is expected to sign a National Security Presidential Directive that White House sources told NBC News was "a game plan to remove al-Qaeda from the face of the Earth." This was largely the same plan that was put into effect after the September 11 attacks.

September 2001—Two US Navy aircraft carrier task forces meet in the Persian Gulf in what would be a normal rotation, but instead of one carrier group replacing the other, both remain in the Gulf. Just before September 11, the United Kingdom was engaged in

Naval maneuvers near Oman with what was billed as the largest armada since the Falklands War. According to international law professor Francis A. Boyle, operation Bright Star was underway in Egypt with 23,000 US troops plus an additional 17,000 from NATO and its associates. This had been planned at least two years ago. NATO also landed 12,000 troops in Turkey. According to Professor Boyle, the war against Afghanistan "had been war-gamed by the Pentagon going back to 1997."

September 3, 2001—The *Times of London* reports that "On September 3 the Federal Aviation Authority made an emergency ruling to prevent Mr. (Salman) Rushdie from flying unless airlines complied with strict and costly security measures. Mr. Rushdie told the *Times* that the airlines would not upgrade their security.

The FAA told the author's publisher that US intelligence had given warning of 'something out there' but failed to give any further details. The FAA confirmed that it stepped up security measures concerning Mr. Rushdie but refused to give any details."

September 5, 2001—Robert Mueller becomes Director of the FBI.

September 6-10, 2001—Unusually large put options, bets that stock prices will fall, are placed on American Airlines and United Airlines stock at the New York Stock Exchange.

September 7, 2001—Florida Governor Jeb Bush signs emergency executive order 01-261 directing the Florida National Guard to work with other police forces and emergency agencies in the event of terrorism.

September 7, 2001—Department of State issues a worldwide caution stating "American citizens may be the target of a terrorist threat from extremist groups with links to Osama bin Laden's al-Qaeda organization...Such individuals have not distinguished between official and civilian targets. As always, we take this information seriously. US Government facilities worldwide remain on heightened alert."

September 7, 2001—In a speech at the Los Angeles Town Hall, Director of Central Intelligence George Tenet says "...we in the intelligence community believe that the chances—even deadly—of surprise are greater now than at any time since the Second World War."

September 7, 2001—According to Mossad expert Gordon Thomas, the CIA receives a message sent by the Mossad's station chief in Washington, Efrain Halevy, warning of the imminent possibility

220

of a massive terrorist attack. Mossad was monitoring and had reportedly even infiltrated al-Qaeda operations in the United States. The secrecy and near blackout by the mainstream US media regarding the FBI dragnet of Israeli spies prior to the terrorist attacks indicates a cover-up. The editor of *Jane's* and others have remarked how surprised that they are the watchdogs have failed to sink their teeth into this story. In May 2002, Thomas says Israeli Prime Minister Ariel Sharon authorized leaks about the September 7 warning, and other warnings, right when Bush faced criticism that the executive knew more than it said it knew.

September 9, 2001—A foreign intelligence service intercepts a telephone call from Osama bin Laden to his stepmother. He warns her, "In two days you're going to hear big news and you're not going to hear from me in a while." US intelligence later denies having evidence that the message existed.

September 10, 2001—Top Pentagon officials, according to *Newsweek* of September 24, 2001, cancel travel plans for the next morning.

September 10, 2001—According to the *New York Times*, Attorney General John Ashcroft submits a budget request that "did not endorse FBI requests for $58 million for 149 new counterterrorism field agents, 200 intelligence analysts and 54

221

additional translators." The *Times* also reported funding cuts in Ashcroft's budget of $65 million for "a program that gives state and local counterterrorism grants and equipment, including radios and decontamination suits and training to localities for counterterrorism preparedness."

September 10, 2001—San Francisco Mayor Willie Brown receives a call, as reported in the *San Francisco Chronicle*, from his airport security personnel warning him not to fly on a scheduled trip from San Francisco to New York September 11.

September 10, 2001—The National Security Agency intercepts two messages indicating, "the match is about to begin," and "tomorrow is zero hour." In June 18, 2002 testimony, NSA Director Lt. General Michael Hayden said the messages were not translated until September 12, 2002.

September 10, 2001—Amr Elgindy cashes out his children's $300,000 trust account. Elgindy would be arrested in May 2002 along with FBI agents Jeffrey Royer and Lynn Wingate who allegedly gave him inside information on the financial dealings of various corporations. Elgindy is a known associate of Adnan Khasshoggi, the infamous arms dealer pardoned by Bush the Elder.

September 11, 2001—Four Boeing jetliners—American Airlines flight 11 and United Airlines flight 175 from Logan International Airport, American Airlines flight 77 from Dulles International Airport, United Airlines flight 93 from Newark International Airport—are skyjacked and crashed into the World Trade Towers, the Pentagon, and a field in Pennsylvania in the worst terrorist attack in US history. In March 2002, US officials said that nine of the skyjackers were selected for special screening at airports before boarding.

7:59am—American Airlines flight 11 leaves Logan Airport in Boston with 92 people on board. Its destination is Los Angeles.

8:01am—United Airlines flight 93 bound for San Francisco is delayed at Newark for forty minutes.

8:13am—Boston ground control loses contact with flight 11 bound for Los Angeles.

8:14am—United Airlines flight 175 departs from Logan. Like American flight 11, it too is bound for Los Angeles.

8:17am—American Airlines flight 77 leaves Dulles Airport in Northern Virginia. It too is bound for Los Angeles.

8:20am—American Airlines flight 11 ceases to emit an IFF signal.

223

8:24am—American Airlines flight 11 broadcasts the following skyjacker message to passengers: "Everything will be ok. If you try to make any moves, you will endanger yourself and the plane. Just stay quiet."

8:25am—Boston ground control notifies other control centers of the skyjacking.

8:28am—American Airlines flight 11 veers sharply out of flight plan to the south. Flight attendant Betty Ong reports skyjacking, adding that two flight attendants and a passenger have been knifed.

8:33am—Skyjacker aboard American Airlines flight 11 tells passengers not to move.

8:38am—Boston ground control informs NORAD (North American Aero-Space Defense Command) that American Airlines flight 11 has been skyjacked. Twenty-five minutes after losing contact with the plane.

8:42am—United Airlines flight 93 departs from Newark for San Francisco.

8:43am—FAA declares United Airlines flight 175 from Logan to Los Angeles hijacked twenty-eight minutes into its flight. The plane turns around over New Jersey and heads towards New York City.

8:45am—American Airlines flight 11 crashes into North Tower of the World Trade Center.

8:46am—United Airlines flight 175 from Logan to Los Angeles ceases to transmit its IFF signal.

8:52am—Two F-15 fighter jets leave Otis Air National Guard Base on Cape Cod.

8:56am—American Airlines flight 77 from Dulles to Los Angeles with sixty-four passengers ceases to emit an IFF signal.

9:00am—American Airlines flight 77 makes a radical turn from its flight path and heads back to Washington, D.C. Flight 77 from Dulles International Airport was known to have been out of control by the FAA since at least 9:00am. Not until 9:24am did NORAD send an alarm to Langley Air Force Base, which is much further away than the obvious choice of scrambling jets from Andrews Air Force Base. Not until 9:30am were two F-16 fighter jet planes scrambled. Standard operating procedure is to immediately scramble jets from Andrews in the case of out of control, skyjacked, or suspicious aircraft that pose potential threats to Washington, D.C.

9:00am—Senator Bob Graham and Representative Porter Goss, both from Florida and members of the two Congressional Intelligence Committees have breakfast in the Capitol with the Chief of Pakistani Intelligence, Lieutenant General Mahmud Ahmad, who would later be fired and placed under house arrest in Pakistan for collaboration with terrorists – he actually funded the operation by giving Atta $100,000 in the summer of 2001.

9:03am—United Airlines flight 175 crashes into the sixtieth floor of the South Tower of the World Trade Center.

9:16am—The FAA announces to NORAD the hijacking of United Airlines flight 93 from Newark to San Francisco.

9:24am—FAA announces the hijacking of American Airlines flight 77. It is tracking a course toward Washington, DC.

9:24am—NORAD initiates the scrambling of three F-16s from Langley Air Force Base in eastern Virginia.

9:30am—A presidential advisor interrupts President Bush while telling a story to a roomful of school children in Sarasota, Florida and whispers that a plane has flown into the World Trade Center.

226

Upon being notified his first call went to Vice President Dick Cheney, then at the White House. His second call went to FBI head Robert Mueller. He then turned to his escort and said, "We're at war."

9:38am—American Airlines flight 77 after pulling out of a downward spiral, whizzes over the treetops of the Army Navy Country Club in south Arlington. As it reaches the top of the hill on the southern edge of Arlington Cemetery, it dips into the plain leading to the Pentagon.

9:40am—In contact with President Bush, Vice President Cheney recommends that United Airlines flight 93, now over Pennsylvania and headed towards Washington D.C., be shot down.

9:40am—Three F-16s take off from Langley Air Force Base one hundred and five miles away from Washington.

9:42am—American Airlines flight 77 crashes into the near empty southwest end of the Pentagon. Jets are finally scrambled from Andrew Air Force Base.

9:45am—The White House is evacuated.

9:57am—President Bush leaves Florida.

227

10:05am—The World Trade Center's south tower collapses.

10:06am—United Airlines flight 93 from Newark to San Francisco crashes or is blown up near Shanksville, Pennsylvania. Pennsylvania state police officials said debris from the plane had been found up to eight miles from the crash site in a residential community where local media have quoted residents as speaking of a second plane in the area and burning debris falling from the sky. *Pittsburgh Post-Gazette* reported that the debris found miles from the site included "clothing, books, papers and what appeared to be human remains."

Reuters ran a story titled "FBI Cannot Rule Out Shootdown of Penn. Plane" by David Morgan September 13, 2001.

One of the passengers of Flight 93, in a cell phone call from the bathroom of the plane, said the plane was going down, heard some sort of explosion, and saw white smoke coming from the plane before contact was lost, according to a report from the Somerset, Pennsylvania county newspaper *Daily American*.

Although flight data and voice tape recorder, the so-called black box, was recovered, the contents have never been made public for independent experts to analyze. Investigators might want to find out whether flight 93 was shot down by the United States Air Force or if the skyjackers had a bomb on board.

10:28am—The World Trade Center's north tower collapses as Federal Buildings in Washington are evacuated.

10:41am—President Bush is on Air Force One en route to Jacksonville, Florida. From there, fighter jets were to escort him to Washington, D.C. But instead he goes to Barksdale Air Force Base in Louisiana, around one o'clock in the afternoon, he records a speech. Vice President Cheney had directed the President to fly to an Air Force base in Louisiana. He then directed the President to fly to Offutt Air Force Base near Omaha, Nebraska, which is the headquarters of the Strategic Air Command. Cheney says, "We've got secure facilities there to update you."

Coincidentally, a charity event was held from 8 am on at Offutt with chief executive officers in attendance who might otherwise have been in their offices in the World Trade Center.[1]

September 12, 2001—On *Good Morning America*, Secretary of State Colin Powell states "I have not seen any evidence that there was a specific signal that we missed."

---

[1] Cheryl Seal "Smoking Gun Five: Final Timeline," *Demcrats.com*.

September 14, 2001—Oil giant Unocal issues the following statement: "The company is not supporting the Taliban in Afghanistan in any way whatsoever. Nor do we have any project or involvement in Afghanistan. Beginning in late 1997, Unocal was a member of a multinational consortium that was evaluating construction of a central Asia gas pipeline between Turkmenistan and Pakistan [via western Afghanistan]. Our company has had no further role in developing or funding that project or any other project that might involve the Taliban."

September 16, 2001—President Bush states "Never (in) anybody's thought process...about how to protect America did we ever think that the evil-doers would fly not one, but four commercial aircraft into precious U.S. targets—never."

September 16, 2001—On *Meet the Press*, Vice President Dick Cheney states "No specific threat involving really a domestic operation or involving what happened, obviously, the cities the airliner and so forth."

September 17, 2001—FBI Director Robert Mueller tells reporters that "there were no warning signs that I'm aware of that would indicate this type of operation in the country."

September 18, 2001—Anthrax letters are mailed to NBC and the *New York Post*. A third letter is probably sent to the National Enquirer in Florida.

September 19-25, 2001—NBC receives and opens anthrax letter.

September 20, 2001—Hoax letters are mailed to NBC and possibly the *New York Post*.

September 25, 2001—NBC receives and opens a hoax letter.

Late September, 2001—Letter reaches Quantico Marine Base accusing former USAMRIID scientist Dr. Asaad of being a terrorist.

October 4, 2001—First report, not publicized, of an anthrax case in a Florida man.

October 4, 2001—British Prime Minister Tony Blair announces in the House of Commons that "a range of people were warned to return back to Afghanistan because of action on or around September 11th."

October 5, 2001—First death by anthrax transpires in Florida.

October 5, 2001—Hoax letters sent to the *New York Times* and *St. Petersburg Times.*

October 5-9, 2001—Hoax letters mailed to CBS in Washington, Fox News and possibly to the *New York Post.*

October 8-13, 2001—Fox News receives hoax letter.

October 9, 2001—Anthrax letters are sent to Daschle and Leahy.

October 12, 2001—New York Times opens hoax letter.

October 12-13, 2001—First media reports surface regarding anthrax attacks.

October 13, 2001—NBC reports anthrax case and suspicious letters.

October 13, 2001—CBS in Washington receives an envelope with powder on the envelope.

October 15, 2001—Daschle's office in the Hart Senate Office Building opens anthrax letter.

October 19, 2001—New York Post anthrax case is diagnosed.

October 26, 2001—President Bush signs the USA Patriot Act into law.

November 9, 2001—Northern Alliance and American forces massacre Taliban and al-Qaeda prisoners at Qala–I–Janghi prison at Mazar-I-Sharif. CIA officer Johnny Spann, inside the prison, is killed in the firefight. So-called American Taliban John Walker Lindh survives and is brought back to stand trial in the United States.

Late November 2001—A hoax letter is mailed from Britain to Daschle's office in the Capitol.

December 21, 2001—In a news briefing, President Bush says "America never dreamt before the September the 11th attacks anybody would attack us."

December 22, 2001—Richard C. Reid tries to light explosives hidden in his shoes aboard an American Airlines flight from Paris to Miami.

January 3, 2002—Daschle's office in the Capitol opens hoax letter.

February 2002—Anthrax vaccine released for use with US troops. BioPort has the exclusive right to make the vaccine.

233

May 12, 2002—Mohammed Alim Razim, minister for Mines and Industries tells Reuters that interim ruler Hamid Karzai used to hold talks with Pakistan and Turkmenistan on Afghanistan's biggest foreign investment project, an 850-kilometer pipeline.

May 16, 2002—In a news briefing at the White House press room, National Security Advisor Condoleezza Rice tells reporters "I don't think anybody could have predicted these people would take an airplane and slam it into the World Trade Center...that they would...use an airplane as a missile."

May 17, 2002—In a Rose Garden ceremony Bush denounces "second-guessing" and says: "Had I known that the enemy was going to use airplanes to kill on that faithful morning, I would have everything in my power to protect the American people."

May 18, 2002—US intelligence officials warn of an al-Qaeda operation as big or bigger than September 11.

May 20, 2002—ABC News reports that the FBI prepares to administer polygraph tests to more than two hundred current and former employees at US Army Medical Research Institute of Infectious Diseases at Fort Deitrick Maryland.

234

May 21, 2002—FBI agent Kenneth Williams testifies that anti-US views at pilot schools prompted his five-page memo identifying a Middle Eastern threat coming from flight schools. Bush spokesman Ari Fleischer concedes that alerts were issued "as a result of all the controversy that took place last week."

May 21, 2002—Senate majority leader Thomas Daschle of South Dakota calls for an independent commission to investigate government action before the September 11 attacks.

May 21, 2002—Law enforcement officials warn of threats to the Brooklyn Bridge and the Statue of Liberty.

May 21, 2002—The World Bank sends workers home and issues antibiotics after a field test reveals possible anthrax contamination.

May 23, 2002—FBI Director Mueller directs an internal investigation on Coleen Rowley's memo as Bush denounces terrorism as the "new totalitarian threat" in Germany's Reichstag.

May 24, 2002—Intelligence reports surface that FBI agent Coleen Rowley has accused a supervisor in Washington, David Frasca, of altering her request for a warrant for Zacorias Moussaoui before the September 11 attacks. According to Rowley, Frasca was later promoted.

235

May 24, 2002—Senators Patrick Leahy (D-Vermont), Charles Grassly (R-Iowa) and Arlen Spector (R-Pennsylvania) write a letter to President Bush seeking a report on pre-September 11 actions. In separate comments, Senator Grassley said on May 25, "This was worse than dropping the ball. This was bureaucrats at headquarters actively interfering with an investigation that had a terrorist in hand."

May 29, 2002—Director of the FBI Robert Mueller acknowledges for the first time that the attacks of September 11 might have been prevented if officials in his agency had responded to available information.

May 30, 2002—The Food and Drug Administration announces that it will allow some drugs and vaccines designed to counter biological, chemical and nuclear terrorism will be approved without being tested in humans to prove effectiveness.

May 30, 2002—The BBC reports Afghanistan, Pakistan, and Turkmenistan have agreed to construct a $2 billion pipeline to bring gas from Central Asia to the subcontinent: "The three countries have agreed to invite international tenders and guarantee funding before launching the project."

June 2002—Judicial Watch announces that it is suing the Bush administration for documents related to the anthrax attacks. The group alleges that because staff were administered Cipro, the White House may have known the attacks were coming and withheld information.

June 1, 2002—In a West Point speech Bush states: "We must take the battle to the enemy, disrupt his plans, and confront the worst threats before they emerge."

June 3, 2002—Federal officials say concerns that racial profiling hindered investigations into Middle Eastern men training at US flight schools.

June 3, 2002—Stanley Hilton, a former aide to Senator Bob Dole, files a $7 billion lawsuit in US District Court against President Bush, Vice President Cheney, National Security Advisor Rice, Secretary of Defense Rumsfeld, and Transportation Secretary Mineta on behalf of the families of 14 victims for "allowing" the attacks to occur. According to the *San Francisco Examiner* (June 11, 2001), Hilton says his sources in the FBI, CIA, NSA, and Naval Intelligence revealed that Bush conspired "to create the Sept. 11 attacks for his own political gain...." The victims' families call their theory LIHOP for Let It Happen on Purpose.

June 4, 2002—Congressional Joint Inquiry committee holds first closed session to probe 9-11 intelligence failure.

June 6, 2002—In a nationally televised prime time address, President George W. Bush announces his proposed to create, "a single, permanent department," at the Cabinet level for homeland security in what he terms, "The most extensive reorganization of the Federal Government since the 1940s." Bush would explain to Congress June 19 that the department would assess threats and map them against vulnerabilities so as to take action and issue warnings and manage the color-coded domestic alert levels. The Homeland Security Act of 2002, as Homeland Security Director Tom Ridge described it to the Senate, called for merging all or parts of twenty-two federal agencies, such as Customs Service, Coast Guard, Immigration and Naturalization Service, into the new department. Responsibilities would be dispersed to more than one hundred entities of the federal government. "This is another opportunity to connect the dots," he said in reference to the department's "competitive analysis" of data supplied by FBI, DEA, INS, and CIA. In presenting its plan, the White House seeks $37.4 billion for its 2003 budget.

June 9, 2002—UnansweredQuestions.org launches website and holds press conference at the National Press Club entitled "9-11 and Public Safety: Seeking Answers and Accountability."

June 10, 2002—US authorities claim to have uncovered the Dirty Bomb plan by José Padilla. Lawmakers and administration officials question alarmist tone of arrest announcement.

June 11, 2002—Widows of the victims of the Trade Center bombings march on Capitol Hill demanding an independent inquiry into the attacks.

June 13, 2002—Traditional council elects Hamed Karzai President of Afghanistan.

June 13, 2002—After an intelligence briefing at the White House, CIA and FBI officials negotiate cease-fire as the Congressional Joint Inquiry Committee stalls over its goals and schedule.

Suggested Reading

Genoa

Insight on the training of Genoa Police can be found in: "Genoa Police Unit Trained by LAPD," *Reuters.* August 7, 2001. For a good overview see: David Graeber's "Among the Thugs: Genoa and the New Language of Protest," *In These Times.* September 3, 2001. For quotes from *La Republica* and *Der Speigel* see: Julie Hyland "Growing international condemnation of police violence in Genoa," *World Socialist Web Site.* August 15, 2001. A first person account can be found in: Wu Ming "The Magical Mystery Tour of the Fake Black Bloc in Genoa," *A-Infos News Service.* Also see John L. Allen, "Fascism's Face in Genoa," *The Nation.* August 15, 2001.

Israel

We were well informed by Howard Schneider's "Blast Kills Ex-Commander Lebanon Massacre," *The Washington Post,* January 25, 2002. Baruch Kimmerling's "I Accuse," in the Israeli Hebrew weekly *Kol Ha'Ir,* February 1, 2002, and Barry Chamish's "Three More Dead In Rabin Coverup Rampage," netvision.net.il. January 15, 2002, remind us that dissent is alive and well in the Holy

Land. Gordon Thomas's "Bush: The Ignored Warning That Will Come to Haunt Him," *Globe-Intel.* May 23, 2002 was highly revealing. We drew on a number of other sources, such as Márcui Carvalho, "CNN Crime Against Public Information," *True Democracy,* fall 2002; the unsigned "Agent Champagne and the Rabin Assassination Mystery," in *Eye Spy,* issue 7, 2002; Christopher Ketchum, "The Israeli 'art student mystery,'" on *salon.com.* May 7, 2002; Paul Rodriguez, "Investigate Report: Intelligence Agents or Art Students?" *Insight on the News,* March 11, 2002; the unsigned "French Reports: U.S. Busts Big Israeli Spy Ring," *Reuters.* March 5, 2002; John Sugg, "Update: The spies who came in from the art sale," *Create Loafing,* March 30, 2002; Carl Cameron and Brit Hume, "Fox News Series on Israeli Spying in the U.S.," *Fox News,* December 2001; Drug Enforcement Agency, "Suspicious Activities Involving Israeli Art Students at DEA Facilities," Formerly classified report. n.d.

Pearl Harbor

Barnes, Harry Elmer in Waller, ed. *Pearl Harbor and the Coming of the War, rev. ed.* Boston: D.C. Heath, 1965.

Beach, Edward L. *Scapegoats: A Defense of Kimmel and Short at Pearl Harbor.* Annapolis: Naval Institute Press, 1995.

Bratzel, John F. and Rout, Leslie B. Jr. "Research Note: Pearl Harbor, Microdots, and J. Edgar Hoover," *American Historical Review, 87.* 1932.

Chamberlin, William H. *America's Second Crusade.* Chicago: Regnery, 1942.

Clausen, Henry C. and Lee, Bruce. *Pearl Harbor: Final Judgement.* n.c.:Da Capo Press, 1992.

Lee, Bruce. *Marching Orders: The Untold Story of World War II.* New York: Crown, 1995.

Morgenstern, George. *Pearl Harbor: The Story of the Secret War.* New York: Devin-Adair, 1947.

Prange, Gordon. *At Dawn We Slept: The Untold Story of Pearl Harbor.* New York: Penguin, 1982.

Rusbridger, James and Nave, Eric. *Betrayal at Pearl* Harbor: *How Churchill Lured Roosevelt into World War II.* New York: Summit Books, 1991.

Stinnet, Robert B. *Day of Deceit: The Truth about Pearl Harbor.* New York: Free Press, 2000.

Tansill, Charles C. *Back Door to War: The Roosevelt Foreign Policy, 1933-1941.* Chicago: Regnery, 1952.

Waller, George M., ed. *Pearl Harbor and the Coming of The War,* rev. ed. Boston: D.C. Heath, 1965.

Bibliography

Ahmed, Rashmee Z. "Bush took FBI agents off Laden family trail," *Times of India.* November 7, 2001.

Alden, Edward. "Storm Warning," *Financial Times.* Weekend May 18/May 19, 2002.

Allen, Mike and Miller, Bill. "Bush Seeks Security Department: Cabinet-Level Agency would Coordinate Anti-Terrorism Effort," *Washington Post.* June 7, 2002.

_____ and Karen DeYoung. "Bush: U.S. Will Strike First at Enemies," *Washington Post,* June 3, 2002.

Anderson, John Lee. "The Assassins: Who was involved in the murder of Ahmed Shah Massoud?," *New Yorker.* June 10, 2002.

Annan, David. "The Assassins and the Knights Templar," in Norman MacKenzie, *Secret Societies,* New York: Crescent Books, Inc., 1967.

Associated Press. "Poll: Many Suspicious of Bush," www.washingtonpost.com. May 21, 2002.

Aurelius, Marcus. *Meditations.* New York: Penguin, 1964.

Balz, Dan. "Bush and GOP Defend White House Response: Democrats on Hill Are Accused of Playing Politics," *Washington Post,* May 18, 2002.

Bamford, James. *Body of Secrets: Anatomy of the Ultra–Secret National Security Agency.* New York: Anchor, 2002.

_____."Too Much, Not Enough," *Washington Post.* June 2, 2002.

Barry, Dan and Baker, Al. "Security Tightened in New York After Vague Threats of Terrorism," *New York Times,* May 22, 2002.

Beesly, Patrick: *Room 40: British Intelligence 1914-18.* New York: Harcourt Brace Jovanovich, 1982.

Boyer, Dave. "Profiling worries called hindrance in terrorism fight: Rights concerns seen as obstacle," The Washington Times, June 4, 2002.

Boyle, Francis A. "Pre-Planned US/UK War Against Afghanistan," *True Democracy.* October 12, 2001.

Bradbery, Angela. "Newly Released Documents Indicate that as Texas Governor, Bush Helped Promote Enron's Business Interests," *Public Citizen Press Release.* February 15, 2002.

Bodansky, Yossef. *Target America.* New York: Shapolsky Publishers, 1993.

Bridis, Ted. "Secret U.S. Court OK'd 934 Warrants," Associated Press. April 30, 2002.

Brisard, Jean-Charles and Dasquié, Guillaume. *Ben Laden: la vérité interdite.* Paris: Denoël, 2001.

Brown, Campbell et al. "What did the White House know,?" www.msnbc.com. May 17, 2002.

Brozzu-Gentile, Jean-Francois. *L'Affaire Gladio: les réseaux secrets américains au coeur du terrorisme en Europe*. Paris: Albin Michel, 1994.

Brzezinski, Matthew. "Bust And Boom," *Washington Post Magazine*. December 30, 2001.

Brzezinkski, Zbigniew. *Grand Chessboard: American Primacy and Its Geostrategic Imperitives*. New York: Basic, 1997.

Bumiller, Elisabeth. "U.S. Must Act First To Battle Terror Bush Tells Cadets: A Speech At West Point: He Says the Cold War Strategy of Deterrence Is Outdated Against New Enemies," *New York Times*. June 2, 2002.

Burckhardt, Jacob. *Civilization of the Renaissance in Italy*. New York: Penguin, 1990.

Bykov, Illarion and Israel, Jared. "Guilty For 9-11: Bush, Rumsfeld, Myers," www.truedemocracy.net. November 14, 2002.

Camus, Albert. *The Fall*. New York: Vintage, 1956.

Carr, Caleb. *Lessons of Terror*. New York: Random House, 2002.

Chomsky, Noam. *9-11*. New York: Seven Stories, 2001.

Christic Institute, *Inside the Shadow Government*. The Christic Institute, Washington 1988.

Churchill, Winston. *Thoughts and Adventures*. New York: Scribner's, 1932

Cieszkowski, August von. *Prolégomènes à l'historiosophie*. Paris: Editions Champ Libre, 1973.

Clancy, Tom. *Debt of Honor*. New York: Penguin, 1994.

Clausewitz, Carl von. *On War.* New York: Penguin, 1982.

Clinton, Hillary Rodham. "Remarks Of Senator Hillary Rodham Clinton on 9/11 Warnings," On the Floor of the United States Senate. May 16, 2002.

CNN. "Bush: 'I would have done everything in my power,'" www.cnn.com. May 17, 2002.

Cole, Leonard A. *Clouds of Secrecy: The Army's Germ Warfare Tests over Populated Areas.* Totowa: Rowman & Littlefield, 1988.

Donner, Frank. *Protectors of Privilege: Red Squads and Police Repression in Urban America.* Los Angeles: The University of California Press, 1990.

Drake,Richard. *The Aldo Moro Murder Case.* Cambridge: Harvard, 1995.

Eggen, Dan. "Ashcroft Invokes Religion in U.S. War on Terrorism," *Washington Post.* n.d.

Elliott, Michael. "How The U.S. Missed The Clues," *Time.* May 27, 2002.

FBI Critical Incidence Response Group, National Center for the Analysis of Violent Crime, Amerithrax Press Briefing. Washington, DC, November 9, 2001.

Ferrell, Robert, H. *American Diplomacy.* New York: Norton, 1975.

Finn, Peter. "Dutch Government Quits After Report on Serb Massacre," *Washington Post.* April 17, 2002.

Freed, Donald and Landis, Fred. *Death in Washington.* Westport: Lawrence Hill, 1980.

Freeman, Clive. "Documentary of US 'war crimes' shocks Europe," *Independent*, June 12, 2002.

Friedman, Alan. *Secret History of How the White House Illegally Armed Iraq*. New York: Bantam, 1993.

Geifman, Anna. *Entangled in Terror: The Azef Affair and the Russian Revolution*. Wilmington: SR Books, 2000.

Gellman, Barton. "A Strategy's Cautious Evolution: Before Sept. 11, the Bush Anti-Terror Effort Was Mostly Ambition," *www.washingtonpost.com*. January 20, 2002.

Gephardt, Richard. "Gephardt on Reports of Bush Knowledge of Al Qaeda Hijackings," News From the House Democratic Leader Press Release. May 16, 2002.

Goddard, Ian Williams. "Government's Prior Knowledge of the OK City Bombing" *Prevailing Winds Magazine* Number Five, 10.

Goldstein, Avram. "IMF-World Bank Anthrax Response Causes Furor," *Washington Post*, May 22, 2002.

Herman, Edward. *Real Terror Network*. Boston: South End Press, 1982.

Hersh, Seymour M. "Missed Messages: Why the government didn't know what it knows," *New Yorker*. June 3, 2002.

Hirsh, Michael and Isikoff, Michael. "What Went Wrong," *Newsweek*, May 27, 2002.

Hodgart, Alan. *Economics of European Imperialism*, New York; Norton, 1977.

Hoffman, David. *Oklahoma City Bombing and the Politics of Terror.* Venice, CA: Feral House, 1998.

Höhne, Heinz. *Order of Death's Head,* New York: Penguin, 2001.

Hutcheson, Ron. "Washington sees unsavory allies: Uzbekistan's leader, who visited the White House, is not big on human rights," *Philadelphia Inquirer.* March 13, 2002.

Isikoff, Michael. "Unheeded warnings: FBI agent's notes pointed to possible World Trade Center attack," www.msnbc.com. May 20, 2002.

Jeffreys-Jones, Rhodri. *Cloak and Dollar: A History of American Secret Intelligence.* New Haven: Yale, 2002.

Johnston, David and Natta, Don Van Jr. "Congressional Inquiry Into 9/11 Will Look Back as Far as 1986," *New York Times,* June 5, 2002.

_____. "Wary of Risk, Slow to Adapt, F.B.I Stumbles in Terror War," *The New York Times,* June 2, 2002.

_____. "FBI Inaction Blurred Picture Before Sept. 11," *The New York Times.* May 27, 2002.

Johnston, David and Becker, Elizabeth. "CIA Was Tracking Hijacker Months Earlier Than It Had Said: Like FBI, Agency Did Not Share Its Intelligence," *The New York Times,* June 3, 2002.

Jones, Archer. *Art of War in the Western World.* Oxford: Oxford, 1989.

Jones, Stephen and Israel, Peter. *Others Unknown: Timothy McVeigh and the Oklahoma City Bombing Conspiracy*. New York: PublicAffairs, 1998.

Keith, Jim. *Biowarfare in America*. Atlanta: Inet, 1999.

_____. *OKbomb!* Lilburn, Georgia: I-Net, 1995.

_____, ed. *Secret and Suppressed: Banned Ideas & Hidden History*.
Portland: Feral House, 1993.

Kiefer, David. "S.F. attorney: Bush allowed 9/11," *The Examiner*. June 11, 2002.

King, John and Barrett, Ted. "White House: 9/11 warnings too vague to help," www.cnn.com. May 16, 2002.

Lane, Mark and Gregory, Dick. *Murder in Memphis: The FBI and the Assassination of Martin Luther King*. New York: Thunder's Mouth, 1993.

Lebert, Stephen and Thomma, Norbert. "Da sind Spuren wie von einer trampelnden Elefantendherde," *Tagesspiegel*, January 13, 2002.

Le Bras-Chopard, Armelle. *La guerre: théologies et idéologies*. Paris: Montchrestien, 1994.

Leiby, Richard. "A Cloak But No Dagger," *Washington Post*, May 18, 2002.

Lewis, Neil. "FBI Chief Admits 9/11 Might Have Been Detectable," *New York Times*, May 30, 2002.

Machiavelli, Niccolò. *The Art of War*. New York: Penguin, 1995.

_____. *The Discourses*. New York: Penguin, 1983.

_____. *The Prince*. New York: Penguin, 1999.

Mann, Robert. *A Grand Delusion: America's Descent into Vietnam.* New York: Basic, 2001.

Martin, Al. *The Conspirators: Secrets of an Iran-Contra Insider.* Pray, Montana: National Liberty Press, 2001.

Mathey, Jean-Marie. *Comprendre la stratégie.* Paris: Economica, 1995.

McGee, Jim. "Briefcase Closed: In Tom Pickard's Retirement as FBU Deputy Director, a Departure With a Difference," *The Washington Post,* February 18, 2002.

McKay, Neil et al. "CIA evidence 'clears Libya' of Lockerbie," *Sunday Herald,* March 3, 2002.

Miller, Judith et al. *Germs: Biological Weapons and America's Secret War.* New York: Simon & Schuster, 2001.

Mitchell, Alison. "Daschle Is Seeking A Special Inquiry on Sept. 11 Attack," *New York Times,* May 22, 2002.

n.a., "The Lion Clawed," *Economist,* September 15, 2001.

National Public Radio. Interview with David Shippers on FBI agent Robert Wright. May 29, 2002.

Natta, Don Van Jr. "Bush Policies Have Been Good to Energy Industry," *New York Times,* April 21, 2002.

Newton, Christopher. "Some Pre-Sept. 11 Documents Released," Associated Press. May 22, 2002.

Nichols, James D. *Freedom's End: Conspiracy in Oklahoma.* Decker: Freedom's End, 1997.

Nichols, John. "McKinney Redux," www.thenation.com, June 10, 2002.

O'Reilly, Bill. "Interview with Larry Johnson cited in Anti-Terror Prober: OKC Bombing Suspect Worked at 9-11 Airport," www.*NewsMax.com*. May 7, 2002.

Palast, Greg. "Has Someone Been Sitting On The FBI,?" BBC Newsnight. November 6, 2001.

_____.and Pallister, David. "FBI claims Bin Laden inquiry was frustrated," *London Guardian*. November 6, 2001.

Pepper, William F. *Orders to Kill: The Truth Behind the Murder of Martin Luther King*. New York: Carroll & Graf, 1995.

Pfaff, William. "American Destiny: Safe for the rest of the world,?" *Commonweal*. May 17, 2002.

Pincus, Walter. "No Link Between Hijacker, Iraq Found, U.S. Says," *Washington Post*. May 1, 2002.

_____. "CIA Gave FBI Warning On Hijacker," *Washington Post*, June 4, 2002.

_____ and Priest, Dana. "CIA Analysts To Help FBI Shift Focus: Terrorism Prevention Key to New Approach," *Washington Post*. May 26, 2002.

Pollack, Andrew and Broad, William. "Antiterror Drugs Get Test Shortcut," *New York Times*, May 31, 2002.

Polybius. *Rise of the Roman Empire*. London: Penguin Books, 1979.

n.a."Prelude: U.S. Intelligence- 11 September 2001," *Eye Spy*. Issue Eight 2002.

Ramsay, Robin. *Conspiracy Theories*. Harpenden: Pocket Essentials, 2000.

Rashid, Ahmed. *Taliban*. New Haven: Yale, 2000.

Ratnesar, Romesh and Weisskopf. "How the FBI Blew the Case," *Time. June 3, 2002.*

Raum, Tom. "Iran-Contra figures get jobs in Bush Administration," *Independent.co.uk,* March 13, 2002.

Reich, Stephanie. "Slow Motion Holocaust: U.S. Designs on Iraq," *Covert Action Quarterly,* Spring 2002.

Risen, James. "Sept. 11 Suspect May Be Relative of '93 Plot Leader: A New Finding On Links: U.S. Officials Say Kuwaiti Had Pivotal Role in Planning the Attacks Last Year," *New York Times,* June 5, 2002.

_____. "Rifts Plentiful as 9/11 Inquiry Begins Today," *New York Times,* June 4, 2002.

_____. "FBI Agent Says Superior Altered Report, Foiling Inquiry," *New York Times,* May 25, 2002.

_____ and Johnston, David. "U.S. Intercepting Messages Hinting at a New Attack," *New York Times,* May 19, 2002.

_____ . "Agent Complaints Lead FBI Director to Ask For Inquiry," *New York Times,* May 24, 2002.

Rondo, Cameron. *Concise Economic History of the World.* New York: Oxford University Press, 1989.

Rosenberg, Barbara. *Analysis of the Anthrax Attacks.* (SUNY-Purchase, February 5, 2002.

Rothkopf, Douglas. "Business Goes To War: How corporations, venture capitalists, and high-tech start-ups can win the war against terror," *Foreign Policy,* May/June 2002.

Rowley, Coleen. "Coleen Rowley's Memo to FBI director Robert Mueller: An edited version of the agent's 13-page letter," *Published in* www.time.com, May 21, 2002.

Rozen, Laura. "Is a U.S. bioweapons scientist behind last fall's anthrax attacks?" *Salon.com,*February 8, 2002.

Ruppert, Mike C."(The) Case for Bush Administration Advance Knowledge of 911 Attacks," *From The Wilderness Publications,* April 22, 2002.

_____. "Timeline Surrounding September "Timeline Surrounding September 11—If CIA And The Government Weren't Involved In the September 11 Attacks What Were They Doing,?" *From The Wilderness Publications.* February 11, 2002.

_____. *(The) Truth and Lies of 9-11.* Sherman Oaks: From the Wilderness Publications, 2002.

_____. "What the CIA Doesn't Want You To Know—Vreeland Interview," *From The Wilderness Publications.* April 4, 2002.

Sanger, David. "In Reichstag, Bush Condemns Terror as New Despotism," *New York Times,* May 24, 2002.

Sanguinetti, Gianfranco. *On Terrorism and the State.* London: Chronos, 1982.

_____. *The Real Report on the Last Chance to Save Capitalism in Italy.* Fort Bragg: Flatland, 1997.

Savinkok, Boris. *Souvenirs d'un terroriste.* Paris: Champ Libre, 1982.

Seal, Cheryl. "Smoking Gun 5: Final Timeline: The Events, Planes and Players of September 11: Putting It All Together," www.democrats.com. n.d.

Simpson, Christopher. *Science of Coercion: Communication Research &* *Psychological Warfare 1945-1960.* New York: Oxford, 1994.

Simpson, Colin. *Lusitania.* New York: Penguin, 1983.

Stafford, Ned. "Newspaper: Echelon Gave Authorities Warning Of Attacks," *From The Wilderness Publications.* September 14, 2001.

Stellin, Susan, "Who's Watching? No, Who's Listening In?" *New York Times,* June 3, 2002.

Suetonius. *The Twelve Cæsars.* Middlesex: Penguin, 1957.

Tzu, Sun. *Art of War.* New York: Oxford, 1963.

UnansweredQuestions.org. "9-11 and the Public Safety: Seeking Answers and Accountability," June 9, 2002. press conference transcript.

United States. *Foreign Relations of the United States.* Washington, D.C.: Government Printing Office, 1915.

Vulliamy, Ed. "Venezuela coup linked to Bush team: Specialists in the 'dirty wars' of the Eighties encouraged the plotters who tried to topple President Chavez," *Observer,* April 21, 2002.

Waldman, Peter and McMorris, Frances A. "The Other Trial: As Sheik Omar Case Nears End, Neither Side Looks Like a Winner," *Wall Street Journal,* September 22, 1995.

Washington Post Staff Writers. "Bush cites CIA-FBI Breakdown: House-Senate Panel Starts Probing 9/11 Intelligence Failure," *Washington Post.* June 5, 2002.

Watson, Dale. "The Terrorist Threat Confronting the United States," Testimony before the Senate Select Committee on Intelligence, February 6, 2002.

Wehrfritz, George et al. "Alleged Hijackers May Have Trained at U.S. Bases," *Newsweek,* September 15, 2001.

White, Jerry. "White House lied about threat to Air Force One," *www.truedemocracy.net.* September 28, 2001. (Cites reports in CBS News and Washington Post)

Willan, Philip. *Puppetmasters: The Political Use of Terrorism in Italy.* London: Constable, 1991.

_____. "Terrorists 'helped by CIA' to stop rise of left in Italy," *Guardian,* March 26, 2001.

Yardley, Jim and Thomas, Jo. "For Agent in Phoenix, the Cause of Many Frustrations Extended to His Own Office, *New York Times,* June 19, 2001.

Index

Halliburton, 99, 114,
137, 182, 190
Hamas, 120
Hanjour, Hani, 104,
106
Hanson, John, 205
Hanssen, Robert, 41
Harari, Michael, 123
Harken, 190
Hart Senate Office
Building, 232
Hartford Courant, 3,
164
Hatfield. J.H., 11, 99
Hatfill, Steven J., 162,
163, 164
Hawaii, 70, 71, 72
Hayden, Michael, 222
Hearst, William
Randolph, 60, 195
Heather, Randall, 205
Hegel, G.W.F., 187,
188
Helms, Jesse, 168
Helms, Richard, 197
Henry, 51, 71, 127,
243
Herodotus, 35
Hersh, Seymor, 200,
113, 216
Hiero of Syracuse, 28
Highway of Death,
131
Hilton, Stanley, 237
Hindenburg, 44
Hiroshima, 76
Hitler, Adolf, 44, 52,
75, 76, 79, 176, 195
Hobbes, Thomas, 175
Hoffman, David, 3, 23,
82, 86
Holocaust, 76, 131,
132, 254
Homeland Security
Act, 238
Honduras, 107
Hoover, J. Edgar, 69,
109, 242

House Un-American
Activities
Committee, 197
Houston, 140, 180,
182, 188, 207
Howe, Carol, 83, 84
Hulagu, 50
Human Rights Watch,
184
Hume, Brit, 124, 242
Hussein, Saddam, 7,
130

I

ibn Husayn, Ali, 126,
127
Illuminati, 189
India, 103, 136, 138,
143, 183, 184, 211,
213, 245
indirect defensive
attack, 39, 73, 80,
88, 96, 125, 130
Information Circular
(IC), 212
Insight, 123, 163, 241,
242
International Civil
Aviation
Organization, 60
Interpol, 82, 111
Iran, 7, 12, 42, 77, 92,
107, 112, 114, 118,
171, 175, 203, 206,
210, 213, 252, 254
Iran-Contra, 42, 77,
107, 171, 203, 252,
254
Iraq, 54, 76, 77, 79,
82, 83, 127, 131,
132, 150, 153, 155,
162, 185, 203, 249,
253, 254
Ireland, 52, 67
Irish Republican Army
(IRA), 38
Isaia, 125, 126
Ismail, 49

266

Peres, Shimon, 54
Peters, Troy, 139
Philadelphia Inquirer, 208, 250
Philippines, 194, 203, 204
Phoenix, 53, 104, 105, 108, 215, 257
Phoenix Program, 53
Pickard, Thomas, 109, 211
Pinochet, 113
pipeline, 29, 93, 99, 100, 114, 128, 129, 136, 137, 138, 140, 141, 142, 183, 184, 207, 230, 234, 236
Pittsburgh Post-Gazette, 228
Plutarch, 47, 48
Poindexter, John, 107
Poland, 195
Polk, James K., 129
Polo, Marco, 48
Polyibus, 193, 253
Pompey, 47, 48
Pope John Paul II, 41
Popular Front for the Liberation of Palestine (PFLP), 54, 55, 112
Pothinus, 185
Powell, Colin, 103, 211, 229
Powers, Tyrone, 135
Presidential Daily Brief (PDB), 216
Prevailing Winds, 3, 82, 83, 87, 88, 249
Prince of Tyre, 49
Project Bojinka, 118
Public Health Security and Bioterrorism Act, 172
Pulitzer, Joseph, 195
Putin, Vladimir, 217

Q

Quantico Marine Base, 156, 231

R

Rabin, 54, 126, 241
Rahman Yassin, Abdul, 23
Rahman, Omar Abdul, 105
Rashid, Ahmed, 3, 137, 180
Rather, Dan, 159
Ravachol, 51
Ray, James Earl, 168
Razim, Mohammed Alim, 234
Reagan, Ronald, 7, 40, 76, 81, 177, 190, 196, 211
Red Brigades, 39, 55, 57
Reed, Fred, 163
Reich, Otto, 107
Reich, Stephanie, 3, 131
Reid, Richard C., 233
Reign of Terror, 75
Reinhart, Tanya, 125
Remington, Frederick, 195
Republican Guard, 83
Republican Party, 153, 190
Resnick, Michael, 120
Ressam, Ahmed, 209, 210
Reuters, 139, 161, 162, 197, 228, 234, 241, 242
Rhodesia, 162
Rice, Condoleeza, 94, 213
Ridge, Tom, 238
Ridley, Yvonne, 28
Riebling, Mark, 174
Robespierre, 46, 47

U

U.S. Army Medical Research Institute for Infectious Diseases (USAMRIID), 148, 150, 156, 163, 167, 231
U.S.S. Cole, 110, 111
Umberto, 52
UnansweredQuestions. org, 3, 42, 103, 139, 238, 256
Union Banking Corporation, 189
United Airlines flight 175, 223, 225, 226
United Airlines flight 93, 119, 223, 224, 226, 227, 228
United Nations (UN), 91, 94, 107, 150, 151, 162
Unocal, 100, 136, 138, 140, 207, 211, 230
USA Patriot Act, 81, 158, 173, 233
USS Maine, 194
Uzbekistan, 92, 114, 136, 137, 140, 213, 250

V

Vailland, 51
Vajpayee, 136
Vatican, 55
Vendrell, Fransesc, 93
Venezuela, 76, 256
Venice Beach, Florida, 42, 107
Vietnam, 53, 74, 130, 134, 177, 199, 252
Virginia, 34, 41, 102, 122, 156, 171, 223, 226
Vogel, Dan, 83
Voice of America, 24, 178

VX gas, 199

W

Waco, 144
Wagner, Clayton Lee, 148, 165
Wahab, 128
Wali-Khan, 203
War on Terrorism, 132, 248
Washington Post, 22, 30, 104, 109, 123, 144, 153, 197, 199, 206, 218, 241, 245, 246, 247, 248, 249, 251, 252, 253, 256, 257
Washington Times, 121, 123, 163, 246
Washington, D.C., 9, 17, 22, 23, 28, 30, 56, 58, 59, 64, 70, 72, 78, 94, 96, 97, 98, 101, 104, 109, 113, 116, 119, 121, 122, 123, 144, 150, 153, 157, 163, 168, 171, 172, 177, 178, 183, 186, 195, 196, 197, 198, 199, 206, 208, 213, 215, 218, 220, 225, 226, 227, 229, 232, 235, 241, 245, 246, 247, 248, 249, 250, 251, 252, 253, 256, 257
Weishaupt, Adam, 189
West Bank, 29
West Point, 132, 185, 237, 247
White House, 17, 25, 36, 69, 102, 107, 109, 116, 130, 144, 153, 160, 165, 167, 173, 179, 181, 191, 200, 204, 209, 211, 214, 218, 227, 234, 237, 238, 239, 245,

Len Bracken may be contacted at:
PO Box 5585
Arlington, VA 22205   USA

Kenn Thomas may be contacted at:

Steamshovel Press
PO Box 210553
St. Louis, MO   63121   USA
$7 for a sample issue
or $25 to get a four issue subscription

or go to: www.steamshovelpress.com

CONSPIRACY & HISTORY

THE SHADOW GOVERNMENT
9-11 and State Terror
by Len Bracken, introduction by Kenn Thomas

Bracken presents the alarming yet convincing theory that nation-states engage in or allow terror to be visited upon their citizens. It is not just liberation movements and radical groups that deploy terroristic tactics for offensive ends. States use terror defensively to directly intimidate their citizens and to indirectly attack themselves or harm their citizens under a false flag. Their motives? To provide pretexts for war or for increased police powers or both. This stratagem of indirectly using terrorism has been executed by statesmen in various ways but tends to involve the pretense of blind eyes, misdirection, and cover-ups that give statesmen plausible deniability. Lusitiania, Pearl Harbor, October Surprise, the first World Trade Center bombing, the Oklahoma City bombing and other well-known incidents suggest that terrorism is often and successfully used by states in an indirectly defensive way to take the offensive against enemies at home and abroad. Was 9-11 such an indirect defensive attack?.
288 PAGES. 6x9 PAPERBACK. ILLUSTRATED. $16.00. CODE: SGOV

POPULAR PARANOIA
The Best of Steamshovel Press
edited by Kenn Thomas

The anthology exposes the biologocal warfare origins of AIDS; the Nazi/Nation of Islam link; the cult of Elizabeth Clare Prophet; the Oklahoma City bombing writings of the late Jim Keith, as well as an article on Keith's own strange death; the conspiratorial mind of John Judge; Marion Pettie and the shadowy Finders group in Washington, DC; demonic iconography; the death of Princess Diana, its connection to the Octopus and the Saudi aerospace contracts; spies among the Rajneeshis; scholarship on the histoirc Illuminati; and many other parapolitical topics. The book also includes the Steamshovel's last-ever interviews with the great Beat writers Allen Ginsberg and William S. Burroughs, and neuronaut Timothy Leary, and new views of the master Beat, Neal Cassady and Jack Kerouac's science fiction.
308 PAGES. 8x10 PAPERBACK. ILLUSTRATED. $19.95. CODE: POPA

THE HISTORY OF THE KNIGHTS TEMPLARS
The Temple Church and the Temple
by Charles G. Addison, introduction by David Hatcher Childress

Chapters on the origin of the Templars, their popularity in Europe and their rivalry with the Knights of St. John, later to be known as the Knights of Malta. Detailed information on the activities of the Templars in the Holy Land, and the 1312 AD suppression of the Templars in France and other countries, which culminated in the execution of Jacques de Molay and the continuation of the Knights Templars in England and Scotland; the formation of the society of Knights Templars in London, and the rebuilding of the Temple in 1816. Plus a lengthy intro about the lost Templar fleet and its connections to the ancient North American sea routes.
395 PAGES. 6x9 PAPERBACK. ILLUSTRATED. $16.95. CODE: HKT

ARKTOS
The Myth of the Pole in Science, Symbolism, and Nazi Survival
by Joscelyn Godwin

A scholarly treatment of catastrophes, ancient myths and the Nazi Occult beliefs. Explored are the many tales of an ancient race said to have lived in the Arctic regions, such as Thule and Hyperborea. Progressing onward, the book looks at modern polar legends including the survival of Hitler, German bases in Antarctica, UFOs, the hollow earth, Agartha and Shambala, more.
220 PAGES. 6x9 PAPERBACK. ILLUSTRATED. $16.95. CODE: ARK

DARK MOON
Apollo and the Whistleblowers
by Mary Bennett and David Percy

•Did you know a second craft was going to the Moon at the same time as Apollo 11?
•Do you know there are serious discrepancies in the account of the Apollo 13 'accident'?
•Did you know that 'live' color TV from the Moon was not actually live at all?
•Did you know that the Lunar Surface Camera had no viewfinder?
•Do you know that lighting was used in the Apollo photographs—yet no lighting equipment was taken to the Moon? All these questions, and more, are discussed in great detail by British researchers Bennett and Percy in Dark Moon, the definitive book (nearly 600 pages) on the possible faking of the Apollo Moon missions. Bennett and Percy delve into every possible aspect of this beguiling theory, one that rocks the very foundation of our beliefs concerning NASA and the space program. Tons of NASA photos analyzed for possible deceptions.
568 PAGES. 6x9 PAPERBACK. ILLUSTRATED. BIBLIOGRAPHY. INDEX. $25.00. CODE: DMO

A HITCHHIKER'S GUIDE TO ARMAGEDDON
by David Hatcher Childress

With wit and humor, popular Lost Cities author David Hatcher Childress takes us around the world and back in his trippy finalé to the Lost Cities series. He's off on an adventure in search of the apocalypse and end times. Childress hits the road from the fortress of Megiddo, the legendary citadel in northern Israel where Armageddon is prophesied to start. Hitchhiking around the world, Childress takes us from one adventure to another, to ancient cities in the deserts and the legends of worlds before our own. Childress muses on the rise and fall of civilizations, and the forces that have shaped mankind over the millennia, including wars, invasions and cataclysms. He discusses the ancient Armageddons of the past, and chronicles recent Middle East developments and their ominous undertones. In the meantime, he becomes a cargo cult god on a remote island off New Guinea, gets dragged into the Kennedy Assassination by one of the "conspirators," investigates a strange power operating out of the Altai Mountains of Mongolia, and discovers how the Knights Templar and their off-shoots have driven the world toward an epic battle centered around Jerusalem and the Middle East.
320 PAGES. 6x9 PAPERBACK. ILLUSTRATED. BIBLIOGRAPHY. INDEX. $16.95. CODE: HGA

24 hour credit card orders—call: 815-253-6390 fax: 815-253-6300
email: auphq@frontiernet.net   www.adventuresunlimitedpress.com   www.wexclub.com

CONSPIRACY & HISTORY

LIQUID CONSPIRACY
JFK, LSD, the CIA, Area 51 & UFOs
by George Piccard

Underground author George Piccard on the politics of LSD, mind control, and Kennedy's involvement with Area 51 and UFOs. Reveals JFK's LSD experiences with Mary Pinchot-Meyer. The plot thickens with an ever expanding web of CIA involvement, from underground bases with UFOs seen by JFK and Marilyn Monroe (among others) to a vaster conspiracy that affects every government agency from NASA to the Justice Department. This may have been the reason that Marilyn Monroe and actress-columnist Dorothy Kilgallen were both murdered. Focusing on the bizarre side of history, *Liquid Conspiracy* takes the reader on a psychedelic tour de force. This is your government on drugs!
264 PAGES. 6x9 PAPERBACK. ILLUSTRATED. $14.95. CODE: LIQC

INSIDE THE GEMSTONE FILE
Howard Hughes, Onassis & JFK
by Kenn Thomas & David Hatcher Childress

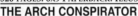

Steamshovel Press editor Thomas takes on the Gemstone File in this run-up and run-down of the most famous underground document ever circulated. Photocopied and distributed for over 20 years, the Gemstone File is the story of Bruce Roberts, the inventor of the synthetic ruby widely used in laser technology today, and his relationship with the Howard Hughes Company and ultimately with Aristotle Onassis, the Mafia, and the CIA. Hughes kidnapped and held a drugged-up prisoner for 10 years; Onassis and his role in the Kennedy Assassination; how the Mafia ran corporate America in the 1960s; the death of Onassis' son in the crash of a small private plane in Greece; Onassis as Ian Fleming's archvillain Ernst Stavro Blofeld; more.
320 PAGES. 6x9 PAPERBACK. ILLUSTRATED. $16.00. CODE: IGF

THE ARCH CONSPIRATOR
Essays and Actions
by Len Bracken

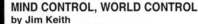

Veteran conspiracy author Len Bracken's witty essays and articles lead us down the dark corridors of conspiracy, politics, murder and mayhem. In 12 chapters Bracken takes us through a maze of interwoven tales from the Russian Conspiracy (and a few "extra notes" on conspiracies) to his interview with Costa Rican novelist Joaquin Gutierrez and his Psychogeographic Map into the Third Millennium. Other chapters in the book are A General Theory of Civil War; A False Report Exposes the Dirty Truth About South African Intelligence Services; The New-Catiline Conspiracy for the Cancellation of Debt; Anti-Labor Day; 1997 with selected Aphorisms Against Work; Solar Economics; and more. Bracken's work has appeared in such pop-conspiracy publications as *Paranoia*, *Steamshovel Press* and the *Village Voice*. Len Bracken lives in Arlington, Virginia and haunts the back alleys of Washington D.C., keeping an eye on the predators who run our country. With a gun to his head, he cranks out his rants for fringe publications and is the editor of *Extraphile*, described by *New Yorker Magazine* as "fusion conspiracy theory."
256 PAGES. 6x9 PAPERBACK. ILLUSTRATED. BIBLIOGRAPHY. $14.95. CODE: ACON.

MIND CONTROL, WORLD CONTROL
by Jim Keith

Veteran author and investigator Jim Keith uncovers a surprising amount of information on the technology, experimentation and implementation of mind control. Various chapters in this shocking book are on early CIA experiments such as Project Artichoke and Project R.H.I.C.-EDOM, the methodology and technology of implants, mind control assassins and couriers, various famous Mind Control victims such as Sirhan Sirhan and Candy Jones. Also featured in this book are chapters on how mind control technology may be linked to some UFO activity and "UFO abductions."
256 PAGES. 6x9 PAPERBACK. ILLUSTRATED. FOOTNOTES. $14.95. CODE: MCWC

NASA, NAZIS & JFK:
The Torbitt Document & the JFK Assassination
introduction by Kenn Thomas

This book emphasizes the links between "Operation Paper Clip" Nazi scientists working for NASA, the assassination of JFK, and the secret Nevada air base Area 51. The Torbitt Document also talks about the roles played in the assassination by Division Five of the FBI, the Defense Industrial Security Command (DISC), the Las Vegas mob, and the shadow corporate entities Permindex and Centro-Mondiale Commerciale. The Torbitt Document claims that the same players planned the 1962 assassination attempt on Charles de Gaul, who ultimately pulled out of NATO because he traced the "Assassination Cabal" to Permindex in Switzerland and to NATO headquarters in Brussels. The Torbitt Document paints a dark picture of NASA, the military industrial complex, and the connections to Mercury, Nevada which headquarters the "secret space program."
258 PAGES. 5x8. PAPERBACK. ILLUSTRATED. $16.00. CODE: NNJ

WHO KILLED DIANA?
by Peter Hounam and Derek McAdam

Hounam and McAdam take the reader through a land of unofficial branches of secret services, professional assassins, Psy-Ops, "Feather Men," remote-controlled cars, and ancient clandestine societies protecting the British establishment. They sort through a web of traceless drugs and poisons, inexplicable caches of money, fuzzy photographs, phantom cars of changing color, a large mysterious dog, and rivals in class and ethnic combat to answer the question, Who Killed Diana?! After this book was published, Mohammed El Fayed held an international news conference to announce that evidence showed that a blinding flash of light had contributed to the crash.
218 PAGES. 6x9 PAPERBACK. ILLUSTRATED. $12.95. CODE: WKD

MIND CONTROL, OSWALD & JFK:
Were We Controlled?
introduction by Kenn Thomas

Steamshovel Press editor Kenn Thomas examines the little-known book *Were We Controlled?*, first published in 1968. The book's author, the mysterious Lincoln Lawrence, maintained that Lee Harvey Oswald was a special agent who was a mind control subject, having received an implant in 1960 at a Russian hospital. Thomas examines the evidence for implant technology and the role it could have played in the Kennedy Assassination. Thomas also looks at the mind control aspects of the RFK assassination and details the history of implant technology. Looks at the case that the reporter Damon Runyon, Jr. was murdered because of this book.
256 PAGES. 6x9 PAPERBACK. ILLUSTRATED. NOTES. $16.00. CODE: MCOJ

PHILOSOPHY & RELIGION

THE TRUTH BEHIND THE CHRIST MYTH
The Redemption of the Peacock Angel
by Mark Amaru Pinkham
Return of the Serpents of Wisdom author Pinkham tells us the Truth Behind the Christ Myth and presents radically new information regarding Jesus Christ and his ancient legend, including: The legend of Jesus Christ is based on a much earlier Son of God myth from India, the legend of Murrugan, the Peacock Angel; The symbol of the Catholic Church is Murrugan's symbol, the peacock, a bird native to southeast Asia; Murrugan evolved into the Persian Mithras, and Mithras evolved into Jesus Christ; Saint Paul came from Tarsus, the center of Mithras worship in Asia Minor. He amalgamated the legend of the Persian Son of God onto Jesus' life story; The Three Wise Men were Magi priests from Persia who believed that Jesus was an incarnation of Mithras; While in India, Saint Thomas became a peacock before he died and merged with Murrugan, the Peacock Angel; The myth of the One and Only Son of God originated with Murrugan and Mithras; The Peacock Angel is a historical figure who has been worshipped by many persons worldwide as The King of the World; Hitler, the Knights Templar, and the Illuminati sought to use the power of the Peacock Angel to conquer the world; more.
174 PAGES. 6x9 PAPERBACK. ILLUSTRATED. BIBLIOGRAPHY. $14.95. CODE: TBCM

CONVERSATIONS WITH THE GODDESS
by Mark Amaru Pinkham
Return of the Serpents of Wisdom author Pinkham tells us that "The Goddess is returning!" Pinkham gives us an alternative history of Lucifer, the ancient King of the World, and the Matriarchal Tradition he founded thousands of years ago. The name Lucifer means "Light Bringer" and he is the same as the Greek god Prometheus, and is different from Satan, who was based on the Egyptian god Set. Find out how the branches of the Matriarchy—the Secret Societies and Mystery Schools—were formed, and how they have been receiving assistance from the Brotherhoods on Sirius and Venus to evolve the world and overthrow the Patriarchy. Learn about the revival of the Goddess Tradition in the New Age and why the Goddess wants us all to reunite with Her now! An unusual book from an unusual writer!
296 PAGES. 7x10 PAPERBACK. ILLUSTRATED. BIBLIOGRAPHY. $14.95. CODE: CWTG.

RETURN OF THE SERPENTS OF WISDOM
by Mark Amaru Pinkham
According to ancient records, the patriarchs and founders of the early civilizations in Egypt, India, China, Peru, Mesopotamia, Britain, and the Americas were colonized by the Serpents of Wisdom—spiritual masters associated with the serpent—who arrived in these lands after abandoning their beloved homelands and crossing great seas. While bearing names denoting snake or dragon (such as Naga, Lung, Djedhi, Amaru, Quetzalcoatl, Adder, etc.), these Serpents of Wisdom oversaw the construction of magnificent civilizations within which they and their descendants served as the priest kings and as the enlightened heads of mystery school traditions. The Return of the Serpents of Wisdom recounts the history of these "Serpents"—where they came from, why they came, the secret wisdom they disseminated, and why they are returning now.
332 PAGES. 6x9 PAPERBACK. ILLUSTRATED. REFERENCES. $16.95. CODE: RSW

THE AQUARIAN GOSPEL OF JESUS THE CHRIST
Transcribed from the Akashic Records
by Levi
First published in 1908, this is the amazing story of Jesus, the man from Galilee, and how he attained the Christ consciousness open to all men. It includes a complete record of the "lost" 18 years of his life, a time on which the New Testament is strangely silent. During this period Jesus travelled widely in India, Tibet, Persia, Egypt and Greece, learning from the Masters, seers and wisemen of the East and the West in their temples and schools. Included is information on the Council of the Seven Sages of the World, Jesus with the Chinese Master Mencius (Meng Tzu) in Tibet, the ministry, trial, execution and resurrection of Jesus.
270 PAGES. 6x9 PAPERBACK. INDEX. $14.95. CODE: AGJC

THE BOOK OF ENOCH
The Prophet
translated by Richard Laurence
This is a reprint of the *Book of Enoch the Prophet* which was first discovered in Abyssinia in the year 1773 by a Scottish explorer named James Bruce. In 1821 *The Book of Enoch* was translated by Richard Laurence and published in a number of successive editions, culminating in the 1883 edition. One of the main influences from the book is its explanation of evil coming into the world with the arrival of the "fallen angels." Enoch acts as a scribe, writing up a petition on behalf of these fallen angels, or fallen ones, to be given to a higher power for ultimate judgment. Christianity adopted some ideas from Enoch, including the Final Judgment, the concept of demons, the origins of evil and the fallen angels, and the coming of a Messiah and ultimately, a Messianic kingdom. The *Book of Enoch* was ultimately removed from the Bible and banned by the early church. Copies of it were found to have survived in Ethiopia, and fragments in Greece and Italy. Like the Dead Sea Scrolls and the Nag Hammadi Library, the *Book of Enoch*, translated from the original Ethiopian Coptic script, is a rare resource that was suppressed by the early church and thought destroyed. Today it is back in print in this expanded, deluxe edition, using the original 1883 revised text.
224 PAGES. 6x9 PAPERBACK. ILLUSTRATED. INDEX. $16.95. CODE: BOE

THE CHRIST CONSPIRACY
The Greatest Story Ever Sold
by Acharya S.
In this highly controversial and explosive book, archaeologist, historian, mythologist and linguist Acharya S. marshals an enormous amount of startling evidence to demonstrate that Christianity and the story of Jesus Christ were created by members of various secret societies, mystery schools and religions in order to unify the Roman Empire under one state religion. In developing such a fabrication, this multinational cabal drew upon a multitude of myths and rituals that existed long before the Christian era, and reworked them for centuries into the religion passed down to us today. Contrary to popular belief, there was no single man who was at the genesis of Christianity; Jesus was many characters rolled into one. These characters personified the ubiquitous solar myth, and their exploits were well known, as reflected by such popular deities as Mithras, Heracles/Hercules, Dionysos and many others throughout the Roman Empire and beyond. The story of Jesus as portrayed in the Gospels is revealed to be nearly identical in detail to that of the earlier savior-gods Krishna and Horus, who for millennia preceding Christianity held great favor with the people.
256 PAGES. 6x9 PAPERBACK. ILLUSTRATED. $16.95. CODE: CHRC

24 hour credit card orders—call: 815-253-6390 fax: 815-253-6300
email: auphq@frontiernet.net   www.adventuresunlimitedpress.com   www.wexclub.com

ANTI-GRAVITY

THE FREE-ENERGY DEVICE HANDBOOK
A Compilation of Patents and Reports
by David Hatcher Childress

A large-format compilation of various patents, papers, descriptions and diagrams concerning free-energy devices and systems. *The Free-Energy Device Handbook* is a visual tool for experimenters and researchers into magnetic motors and other "over-unity" devices. With chapters on the Adams Motor, the Hans Coler Generator, cold fusion, superconductors, "N" machines, space-energy generators, Nikola Tesla, T. Townsend Brown, and the latest in free-energy devices. Packed with photos, technical diagrams, patents and fascinating information, this book belongs on every science shelf. With energy and profit being a major political reason for fighting various wars, free-energy devices, if ever allowed to be mass distributed to consumers, could change the world! Get your copy now before the Department of Energy bans this book!

292 PAGES. 8x10 PAPERBACK. ILLUSTRATED. BIBLIOGRAPHY. $16.95. CODE: FEH

THE ANTI-GRAVITY HANDBOOK
edited by David Hatcher Childress, with Nikola Tesla, T.B. Paulicki, Bruce Cathie, Albert Einstein and others

The new expanded compilation of material on Anti-Gravity, Free Energy, Flying Saucer Propulsion, UFOs, Suppressed Technology, NASA Cover-ups and more. Highly illustrated with patents, technical illustrations and photos. This revised and expanded edition has more material, including photos of Area 51, Nevada, the government's secret testing facility. This classic on weird science is back in a 90s format!
* How to build a flying saucer.
* Arthur C. Clarke on Anti-Gravity.
* Crystals and their role in levitation.
* Secret government research and development.
* Nikola Tesla on how anti-gravity airships could draw power from the atmosphere.
* Bruce Cathie's Anti-Gravity Equation.
* NASA, the Moon and Anti-Gravity.

230 PAGES. 7x10 PAPERBACK. BIBLIOGRAPHY/INDEX/APPENDIX. HIGHLY ILLUSTRATED. $14.95. CODE: AGH

ANTI-GRAVITY & THE WORLD GRID

Is the earth surrounded by an intricate electromagnetic grid network offering free energy? This compilation of material on ley lines and world power points contains chapters on the geography, mathematics, and light harmonics of the earth grid. Learn the purpose of ley lines and ancient megalithic structures located on the grid. Discover how the grid made the Philadelphia Experiment possible. Explore the Coral Castle and many other mysteries, including acoustic levitation, Tesla Shields and scalar wave weaponry. Browse through the section on anti-gravity patents, and research resources.

274 PAGES. 7x10 PAPERBACK. ILLUSTRATED. $14.95. CODE: AGW

ANTI-GRAVITY & THE UNIFIED FIELD
edited by David Hatcher Childress

Is Einstein's Unified Field Theory the answer to all of our energy problems? Explored in this compilation of material is how gravity, electricity and magnetism manifest from a unified field around us. Why artificial gravity is possible; secrets of UFO propulsion; free energy; Nikola Tesla and anti-gravity airships of the 20s and 30s; flying saucers as superconducting whirls of plasma; anti-mass generators; vortex propulsion; suppressed technology; government cover-ups; gravitational pulse drive; spacecraft & more.

240 PAGES. 7x10 PAPERBACK. ILLUSTRATED. $14.95. CODE: AGU

ETHER TECHNOLOGY
A Rational Approach to Gravity Control
by Rho Sigma

This classic book on anti-gravity and free energy is back in print and back in stock. Written by a well-known American scientist under the pseudonym of "Rho Sigma," this book delves into international efforts at gravity control and discoid craft propulsion. Before the Quantum Field, there was "Ether." This small, but informative book has chapters on John Searle and "Searle discs;" T. Townsend Brown and his work on anti-gravity and ether-vortex turbines. Includes a forward by former NASA astronaut Edgar Mitchell.

108 PAGES. 6x9 PAPERBACK. ILLUSTRATED. $12.95. CODE: ETT

TAPPING THE ZERO POINT ENERGY
Free Energy & Anti-Gravity in Today's Physics
by Moray B. King

King explains how free energy and anti-gravity are possible. The theories of the zero point energy maintain there are tremendous fluctuations of electrical field energy imbedded within the fabric of space. This book tells how, in the 1930s, inventor T. Henry Moray could produce a fifty kilowatt "free energy" machine; how an electrified plasma vortex creates anti-gravity; how the Pons/Fleischmann "cold fusion" experiment could produce tremendous heat without fusion; and how certain experiments might produce a gravitational anomaly.

190 PAGES. 5x8 PAPERBACK. ILLUSTRATED. $12.95. CODE: TAP

24 hour credit card orders—call: 815-253-6390 fax: 815-253-6300

email: auphq@frontiernet.net   www.adventuresunlimitedpress.com   www.wexclub.com

FREE ENERGY SYSTEMS

LOST SCIENCE
by Gerry Vassilatos
Rediscover the legendary names of suppressed scientific revolution—remarkable lives, astounding discoveries, and incredible inventions which would have produced a world of wonder. How did the aura research of Baron Karl von Reichenbach prove the vitalistic theory and frighten the greatest minds of Germany? How did the physiophone and wireless of Antonio Meucci predate both Bell and Marconi by decades? How does the earth battery technology of Nathan Stubblefield portend an unsuspected energy revolution? How did the geoaetheric engines of Nikola Tesla threaten the establishment of a fuel-dependent America? The microscopes and virus-destroying ray machines of Dr. Royal Rife provided the solution for every world-threatening disease. Why did the FDA and AMA together condemn this great man to Federal Prison? The static crashes on telephone lines enabled Dr. T. Henry Moray to discover the reality of radiant space energy. Was the mysterious "Swedish stone," the powerful mineral which Dr. Moray discovered, the very first historical instance in which stellar power was recognized and secured on earth? Why did the Air Force initially fund the gravitational warp research and warp-cloaking devices of T. Townsend Brown and then reject it? When the controlled fusion devices of Philo Farnsworth achieved the "break-even" point in 1967 the FUSOR project was abruptly cancelled by ITT.
304 PAGES. 6X9 PAPERBACK. ILLUSTRATED. BIBLIOGRAPHY. $16.95. CODE: LOS

SECRETS OF COLD WAR TECHNOLOGY
Project HAARP and Beyond
by Gerry Vassilatos
Vassilatos reveals that "Death Ray" technology has been secretly researched and developed since the turn of the century. Included are chapters on such inventors and their devices as H.C. Vion, the developer of auroral energy receivers; Dr. Selim Lemstrom's pre-Tesla experiments; the early beam weapons of Grindell-Mathews, Ulivi, Turpain and others; John Hettenger and his early beam power systems. Learn about Project Argus, Project Teak and Project Orange; EMP experiments in the 60s; why the Air Force directed the construction of a huge Ionospheric "backscatter" telemetry system across the Pacific just after WWII; why Raytheon has collected every patent relevant to HAARP over the past few years; more.
250 PAGES. 6X9 PAPERBACK. ILLUSTRATED. $15.95. CODE: SCWT

THE A.T. FACTOR
A Scientists Encounter with UFOs: Piece For A Jigsaw Part 3
by Leonard Cramp
British aerospace engineer Cramp began much of the scientific anti-gravity and UFO propulsion analysis back in 1955 with his landmark book *Space, Gravity & the Flying Saucer* (out-of-print and rare). His next books (available from Adventures Unlimited) *UFOs & Anti-Gravity: Piece for a Jig-Saw* and *The Cosmic Matrix: Piece for a Jig-Saw Part 2* began Cramp's in depth look into gravity control, free-energy, and the interlocking web of energy that pervades the universe. In this final book, Cramp brings to a close his detailed and controversial study of UFOs and Anti-Gravity.
324 PAGES. 6X9 PAPERBACK. ILLUSTRATED. BIBLIOGRAPHY. INDEX. $16.95. CODE: ATF

THE TIME TRAVEL HANDBOOK
A Manual of Practical Teleportation & Time Travel
edited by David Hatcher Childress
In the tradition of *The Anti-Gravity Handbook* and *The Free-Energy Device Handbook*, science and UFO author David Hatcher Childress takes us into the weird world of time travel and teleportation. Not just a whacked-out look at science fiction, this book is an authoritative chronicling of real-life time travel experiments, teleportation devices and more. *The Time Travel Handbook* takes the reader beyond the government experiments and deep into the uncharted territory of early time travellers such as Nikola Tesla and Guglielmo Marconi and their alleged time travel experiments, as well as the Wilson Brothers of EMI and their connection to the Philadelphia Experiment—the U.S. Navy's forays into invisibility, time travel, and teleportation. Childress looks into the claims of time travelling individuals, and investigates the unusual claim that the pyramids on Mars were built in the future and sent back in time. A highly visual, large format book, with patents, photos and schematics. Be the first on your block to build your own time travel device!
316 PAGES. 7X10 PAPERBACK. ILLUSTRATED. $16.95. CODE: TTH

THE TESLA PAPERS
Nikola Tesla on Free Energy & Wireless Transmission of Power
by Nikola Tesla, edited by David Hatcher Childress
David Hatcher Childress takes us into the incredible world of Nikola Tesla and his amazing inventions. Tesla's rare article "The Problem of Increasing Human Energy with Special Reference to the Harnessing of the Sun's Energy" is included. This lengthy article was originally published in the June 1900 issue of *The Century Illustrated Monthly Magazine* and it was the outline for Tesla's master blueprint for the world. Tesla's fantastic vision of the future, including wireless power, anti-gravity, free energy and highly advanced solar power. Also included are some of the papers, patents and material collected on Tesla at the Colorado Springs Tesla Symposiums, including papers on: •The Secret History of Wireless Transmission •Tesla and the Magnifying Transmitter •Design and Construction of a Half-Wave Tesla Coil •Electrostatics: A Key to Free Energy •Progress in Zero-Point Energy Research •Electromagnetic Energy from Antennas to Atoms •Tesla's Particle Beam Technology •Fundamental Excitatory Modes of the Earth-Ionosphere Cavity
325 PAGES. 8X10 PAPERBACK. ILLUSTRATED. $16.95. CODE: TTP

THE FANTASTIC INVENTIONS OF NIKOLA TESLA
by Nikola Tesla with additional material by David Hatcher Childress
This book is a readable compendium of patents, diagrams, photos and explanations of the many incredible inventions of the originator of the modern era of electrification. In Tesla's own words are such topics as wireless transmission of power, death rays, and radio-controlled airships. In addition, rare material on German bases in Antarctica and South America, and a secret city built at a remote jungle site in South America by one of Tesla's students, Guglielmo Marconi. Marconi's secret group claims to have built flying saucers in the 1940s and to have gone to Mars in the early 1950s! Incredible photos of these Tesla craft are included. The Ancient Atlantean system of broadcasting energy through a grid system of obelisks and pyramids is discussed, and a fascinating concept comes out of one chapter: that Egyptian engineers had to wear protective metal head-shields while in these power plants, hence the Egyptian Pharoah's head covering as well as the Face on Mars! •His plan to transmit free electricity into the atmosphere. •How electrical devices would work using only small antennas. •Why unlimited power could be utilized anywhere on earth. •How radio and radar technology can be used as death-ray weapons in Star Wars.
342 PAGES. 6X9 PAPERBACK. ILLUSTRATED. $16.95. CODE: FINT

24 hour credit card orders—call: 815-253-6390 fax: 815-253-6300
email: auphq@frontiernet.net   www.adventuresunlimitedpress.com   www.wexclub.com

ATLANTIS STUDIES

MAPS OF THE ANCIENT SEA KINGS
Evidence of Advanced Civilization in the Ice Age
by Charles H. Hapgood
Charles Hapgood's classic 1966 book on ancient maps produces concrete evidence of an advanced world-wide civilization existing many thousands of years before ancient Egypt. He has found the evidence in the Piri Reis Map that shows Antarctica, the Hadji Ahmed map, the Oronteus Finaeus and other amazing maps. Hapgood concluded that these maps were made from more ancient maps from the various ancient archives around the world, now lost. Not only were these unknown people more advanced in mapmaking than any people prior to the 18th century, it appears they mapped all the continents. The Americas were mapped thousands of years before Columbus. Antarctica was mapped when its coasts were free of ice.
316 PAGES. 7X10 PAPERBACK. ILLUSTRATED. BIBLIOGRAPHY & INDEX. $19.95. CODE: MASK

PATH OF THE POLE
Cataclysmic Pole Shift Geology
by Charles Hapgood
Maps of the Ancient Sea Kings author Hapgood's classic book *Path of the Pole* is back in print! Hapgood researched Antarctica, ancient maps and the geological record to conclude that the Earth's crust has slipped in the inner core many times in the past, changing the position of the pole. *Path of the Pole* discusses the various "pole shifts" in Earth's past, giving evidence for each one, and moves on to possible future pole shifts. Packed with illustrations, this is the sourcebook for many other books on cataclysms and pole shifts.
356 PAGES. 6X9 PAPERBACK. ILLUSTRATED. $16.95. CODE: POP.

ATLANTIS: THE ANDES SOLUTION
The Theory and the Evidence
by J.M. Allen, forward by John Blashford-Snell
Imported from Britain, this deluxe hardback is J.M. Allen's fascinating research into the lost world that exists on the Bolivian Plateau and his theory that it is Atlantis. Allen looks into Lake Titicaca, the ruins of Tiahuanaco and the mysterious Lake PooPoo. The high plateau of Bolivia must contain the remains of Atlantis, claims Allen. Lots of fascinating stuff here with Allen discovering the remains of huge ancient canals that once crisscrossed the vast plain southwest of Tiahuanaco. A must-read for all researchers into South America, Atlantis and mysteries of the past. With lots of illustrations, some in color.
196 PAGES. 6X9 HARDBACK. ILLUSTRATED. BIBLIOGRAPHY. $25.99. CODE: ATAS

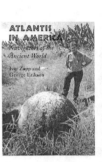

ATLANTIS IN AMERICA
Navigators of the Ancient World
by Ivar Zapp and George Erikson
This book is an intensive examination of the archeological sites of the Americas, an examination that reveals civilization has existed here for tens of thousands of years. Zapp is an expert on the enigmatic giant stone spheres of Costa Rica, and maintains that they were sighting stones similar to those found throughout the Pacific as well as in Egypt and the Middle East. They were used to teach star-paths and sea navigation to the world-wide navigators of the ancient world. While the Mediterranean and European regions "forgot" world-wide navigation and fought wars, the Mesoamericans of diverse races were building vast interconnected cities without walls. This Golden Age of ancient America was merely a myth of suppressed history—until now. Profusely illustrated, chapters are on Navigators of the Ancient World; Pyramids & Megaliths: Older Than You Think; Ancient Ports and Colonies; Cataclysms of the Past; Atlantis: From Myth to Reality; The Serpent and the Cross: The Loss of the City States; Calendars and Star Temples; and more.
360 PAGES. 6X9 PAPERBACK. ILLUSTRATED. BIBLIOGRAPHY & INDEX. $17.95. CODE: AIA

FAR-OUT ADVENTURES   *REVISED EDITION*
The Best of World Explorer Magazine
This is a compilation of the first nine issues of *World Explorer* in a large-format paperback. Authors include: David Hatcher Childress, Joseph Jochmans, John Major Jenkins, Deanna Emerson, Katherine Routledge, Alexander Horvat, Greg Deyermenjian, Dr. Marc Miller, and others. Articles in this book include Smithsonian Gate, Dinosaur Hunting in the Congo, Secret Writings of the Incas, On the Trail of the Yeti, Secrets of the Sphinx, Living Pterodactyls, Quest for Atlantis, What Happened to the Great Library of Alexandria?, In Search of Seamonsters, Egyptians in the Pacific, Lost Megaliths of Guatemala, the Mystery of Easter Island, Comalcalco: Mayan City of Mystery, Professor Wexler and plenty more.
580 PAGES. 8X11 PAPERBACK. ILLUSTRATED. REVISED EDITION. $25.00. CODE: FOA

RETURN OF THE SERPENTS OF WISDOM
by Mark Amaru Pinkham
According to ancient records, the patriarchs and founders of the early civilizations in Egypt, India, China, Peru, Mesopotamia, Britain, and the Americas were the Serpents of Wisdom—spiritual masters associated with the serpent—who arrived in these lands after abandoning their beloved homelands and crossing great seas. While bearing names denoting snake or dragon (such as Naga, Lung, Djedhi, Amaru, Quetzalcoatl, Adder, etc.), these Serpents of Wisdom oversaw the construction of magnificent civilizations within which they and their descendants served as the priest kings and as the enlightened heads of mystery school traditions. *The Return of the Serpents of Wisdom* recounts the history of these "Serpents"—where they came from, why they came, the secret wisdom they disseminated, and why they are returning now.
400 PAGES. 6X9 PAPERBACK. ILLUSTRATED. REFERENCES. $16.95. CODE: RSW

24 hour credit card orders—call: 815-253-6390 fax: 815-253-6300
email: auphq@frontiernet.net   www.adventuresunlimitedpress.com   www.wexclub.com

LOST CITIES

TECHNOLOGY OF THE GODS
The Incredible Sciences of the Ancients
by David Hatcher Childress

Popular *Lost Cities* author David Hatcher Childress takes us into the amazing world of ancient technology, from computers in antiquity to the "flying machines of the gods." Childress looks at the technology that was allegedly used in Atlantis and the theory that the Great Pyramid of Egypt was originally a gigantic power station. He examines tales of ancient flight and the technology that it involved; how the ancients used electricity; megalithic building techniques; the use of crystal lenses and the fire from the gods; evidence of various high tech weapons in the past, including atomic weapons; ancient metallurgy and heavy machinery; the role of modern inventors such as Nikola Tesla in bringing ancient technology back into modern use; impossible artifacts; and more.
356 PAGES. 6X9 PAPERBACK. ILLUSTRATED. BIBLIOGRAPHY. $16.95. CODE: TGOD

VIMANA AIRCRAFT OF ANCIENT INDIA & ATLANTIS
by David Hatcher Childress, introduction by Ivan T. Sanderson

Did the ancients have the technology of flight? In this incredible volume on ancient India, authentic Indian texts such as the *Ramayana* and the *Mahabharata* are used to prove that ancient aircraft were in use more than four thousand years ago. Included in this book is the entire Fourth Century BC manuscript *Vimaanika Shastra* by the ancient author Maharishi Bharadwaaja, translated into English by the Mysore Sanskrit professor G.R. Josyer. Also included are chapters on Atlantean technology, the incredible Rama Empire of India and the devastating wars that destroyed it. Also an entire chapter on mercury vortex propulsion and mercury gyros, the power source described in the ancient Indian texts. Not to be missed by those interested in ancient civilizations or the UFO enigma.
334 PAGES. 6X9 PAPERBACK. RARE PHOTOGRAPHS, MAPS AND DRAWINGS. $15.95. CODE: VAA

LOST CONTINENTS & THE HOLLOW EARTH
I Remember Lemuria and the Shaver Mystery
by David Hatcher Childress & Richard Shaver

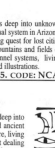

Lost Continents & the Hollow Earth is Childress' thorough examination of the early hollow earth stories of Richard Shaver and the fascination that fringe fantasy subjects such as lost continents and the hollow earth have had for the American public. Shaver's rare 1948 book *I Remember Lemuria* is reprinted in its entirety, and the book is packed with illustrations from Ray Palmer's *Amazing Stories* magazine of the 1940s. Palmer and Shaver told of tunnels running through the earth—tunnels inhabited by the Deros and Teros, humanoids from an ancient spacefaring race that had inhabited the earth, eventually going underground, hundreds of thousands of years ago. Childress discusses the famous hollow earth books and delves deep into whatever reality may be behind the stories of tunnels in the earth. Operation High Jump to Antarctica in 1947 and Admiral Byrd's bizarre statements, tunnel systems in South America and Tibet, the underground world of Agartha, the belief of UFOs coming from the South Pole, more.
344 PAGES. 6X9 PAPERBACK. ILLUSTRATED. $16.95. CODE: LCHE

LOST CITIES OF NORTH & CENTRAL AMERICA
by David Hatcher Childress

Down the back roads from coast to coast, maverick archaeologist and adventurer David Hatcher Childress goes deep into unknown America. With this incredible book, you will search for lost Mayan cities and books of gold, discover an ancient canal system in Arizona, climb gigantic pyramids in the Midwest, explore megalithic monuments in New England, and join the astonishing quest for lost cities throughout North America. Travel from the war-torn jungles of Guatemala, Nicaragua and Honduras to the deserts, mountains and fields of Mexico, Canada, and the U.S.A., Childress takes the reader in search of sunken ruins, Viking forts, strange tunnel systems, living dinosaurs, early Chinese explorers, and fantastic lost treasure. Packed with both early and current maps, photos and illustrations.
590 PAGES. 6X9 PAPERBACK. ILLUSTRATED. FOOTNOTES & BIBLIOGRAPHY. $14.95. CODE: NCA

LOST CITIES & ANCIENT MYSTERIES OF SOUTH AMERICA
by David Hatcher Childress

Rogue adventurer and maverick archaeologist David Hatcher Childress takes the reader on unforgettable journeys deep into deadly jungles, high up on windswept mountains and across scorching deserts in search of lost civilizations and ancient mysteries. Travel with David and explore stone cities high in mountain forests and hear fantastic tales of Inca treasure, living dinosaurs, and a mysterious tunnel system. Whether he is hopping freight trains, searching for secret cities, or just dealing with the daily problems of food, money, and romance, the author keeps the reader spellbound. Includes both early and current maps, photos, and illustrations, and plenty of advice for the explorer planning his or her own journey of discovery.
381 PAGES. 6X9 PAPERBACK. ILLUSTRATED. FOOTNOTES & BIBLIOGRAPHY. $14.95. CODE: SAM

LOST CITIES & ANCIENT MYSTERIES OF AFRICA & ARABIA
by David Hatcher Childress

Across ancient deserts, dusty plains and steaming jungles, maverick archaeologist David Childress continues his worldwide quest for lost cities and ancient mysteries. Join him as he discovers forbidden cities in the Empty Quarter of Arabia; "Atlantean" ruins in Egypt and the Kalahari desert; a mysterious, ancient empire in the Sahara; and more. This is the tale of an extraordinary life on the road: across war-torn countries, Childress searches for King Solomon's Mines, living dinosaurs, the Ark of the Covenant and the solutions to some of the fantastic mysteries of the past.
423 PAGES. 6X9 PAPERBACK. ILLUSTRATED. FOOTNOTES & BIBLIOGRAPHY. $14.95. CODE: AFA

---

24 hour credit card orders—call: 815-253-6390 fax: 815-253-6300
email: auphq@frontiernet.net   www.adventuresunlimitedpress.com   www.wexclub.com

LOST CITIES

LOST CITIES OF ATLANTIS, ANCIENT EUROPE & THE MEDITERRANEAN
by David Hatcher Childress
Atlantis! The legendary lost continent comes under the close scrutiny of maverick archaeologist David Hatcher Childress in this sixth book in the internationally popular *Lost Cities* series. Childress takes the reader in search of sunken cities in the Mediterranean; across the Atlas Mountains in search of Atlantean ruins; to remote islands in search of megalithic ruins; to meet living legends and secret societies. From Ireland to Turkey, Morocco to Eastern Europe, and around the remote islands of the Mediterranean and Atlantic, Childress takes the reader on an astonishing quest for mankind's past. Ancient technology, cataclysms, megalithic construction, lost civilizations and devastating wars of the past are all explored in this book. Childress challenges the skeptics and proves that great civilizations not only existed in the past, but the modern world and its problems are reflections of the ancient world of Atlantis.
524 PAGES. 6x9 PAPERBACK. ILLUSTRATED WITH 100S OF MAPS, PHOTOS AND DIAGRAMS. BIBLIOGRAPHY & INDEX. $16.95. CODE: MED

LOST CITIES OF CHINA, CENTRAL INDIA & ASIA
by David Hatcher Childress
Like a real life "Indiana Jones," maverick archaeologist David Childress takes the reader on an incredible adventure across some of the world's oldest and most remote countries in search of lost cities and ancient mysteries. Discover ancient cities in the Gobi Desert; hear fantastic tales of lost continents, vanished civilizations and secret societies bent on ruling the world; visit forgotten monasteries in forbidding snow-capped mountains with strange tunnels to mysterious subterranean cities! A unique combination of far-out exploration and practical travel advice, it will astound and delight the experienced traveler or the armchair voyager.
429 PAGES. 6x9 PAPERBACK. ILLUSTRATED. FOOTNOTES & BIBLIOGRAPHY. $14.95. CODE: CHI

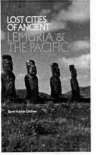

LOST CITIES OF ANCIENT LEMURIA & THE PACIFIC
by David Hatcher Childress
Was there once a continent in the Pacific? Called Lemuria or Pacifica by geologists, Mu or Pan by the mystics, there is now ample mythological, geological and archaeological evidence to "prove" that an advanced and ancient civilization once lived in the central Pacific. Maverick archaeologist and explorer David Hatcher Childress combs the Indian Ocean, Australia and the Pacific in search of the surprising truth about mankind's past. Contains photos of the underwater city on Pohnpei; explanations on how the statues were levitated around Easter Island in a clockwise vortex movement; tales of disappearing islands; Egyptians in Australia; and more.
379 PAGES. 6x9 PAPERBACK. ILLUSTRATED. FOOTNOTES & BIBLIOGRAPHY. $14.95. CODE: LEM

ANCIENT TONGA
& the Lost City of Mu'a
by David Hatcher Childress
Lost Cities series author Childress takes us to the south sea islands of Tonga, Rarotonga, Samoa and Fiji to investigate the megalithic ruins on these beautiful islands. The great empire of the Polynesians, centered on Tonga and the ancient city of Mu'a, is revealed with old photos, drawings and maps. Chapters in this book are on the Lost City of Mu'a and its many megalithic pyramids, the Ha'amonga Trilithon and ancient Polynesian astronomy, Samoa and the search for the lost land of Havai'iki, Fiji and its wars with Tonga, Rarotonga's megalithic road, and Polynesian cosmology. Material on Egyptians in the Pacific, earth changes, the fortified moat around Mu'a, lost roads, more.
218 PAGES. 6x9 PAPERBACK. ILLUSTRATED. COLOR PHOTOS. BIBLIOGRAPHY. $15.95. CODE: TONG

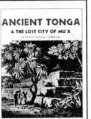

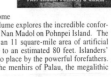

ANCIENT MICRONESIA
& the Lost City of Nan Madol
by David Hatcher Childress
Micronesia, a vast archipelago of islands west of Hawaii and south of Japan, contains some of the most amazing megalithic ruins in the world. Part of our *Lost Cities* series, this volume explores the incredible conformations on various Micronesian islands, especially the fantastic and little-known ruins of Nan Madol on Pohnpei Island. The huge canal city of Nan Madol contains over 250 million tons of basalt columns over an 11 square-mile area of artificial islands. Much of the huge city is submerged, and underwater structures can be found to an estimated 80 feet. Islanders' legends claim that the basalt rocks, weighing up to 50 tons, were magically levitated into place by the powerful forefathers. Other ruins in Micronesia that are profiled include the Latte Stones of the Marianas, the menhirs of Palau, the megalithic canal city on Kosrae Island, megaliths on Guam, and more.
256 PAGES. 6x9 PAPERBACK. ILLUSTRATED. INCLUDES A COLOR PHOTO SECTION. BIBLIOGRAPHY. $16.95. CODE: AMIC

24 hour credit card orders—call: 815-253-6390 fax: 815-253-6300
email: auphq@frontiernet.net   www.adventuresunlimitedpress.com   www.wexclub.com

One Adventure Place
P.O. Box 74
Kempton, Illinois 60946
United States of America
•Tel.: 1-800-718-4514 or 815-253-6390
•Fax: 815-253-6300
Email: auphq@frontiernet.net
http://www.adventuresunlimitedpress.com
or www.adventuresunlimited.nl

10% Discount when you order 3 or more items!

ORDERING INSTRUCTIONS

✓ Remit by USD$ Check, Money Order or Credit Card
✓ Visa, Master Card, Discover & AmEx Accepted
✓ Prices May Change Without Notice
✓ 10% Discount for 3 or more Items

SHIPPING CHARGES

United States

✓ Postal Book Rate { $3.00 First Item
50¢ Each Additional Item
✓ Priority Mail { $4.50 First Item
$2.00 Each Additional Item
✓ UPS { $5.00 First Item
$1.50 Each Additional Item
NOTE: UPS Delivery Available to Mainland USA Only

Canada

✓ Postal Book Rate { $6.00 First Item
$2.00 Each Additional Item
✓ Postal Air Mail { $8.00 First Item
$2.50 Each Additional Item
✓ Personal Checks or Bank Drafts MUST BE
USD$ and Drawn on a US Bank
✓ Canadian Postal Money Orders OK
✓ Payment MUST BE USD$

All Other Countries

✓ Surface Delivery { $10.00 First Item
$4.00 Each Additional Item
✓ Postal Air Mail { $14.00 First Item
$5.00 Each Additional Item
✓ Payment MUST BE USD$
✓ Checks and Money Orders MUST BE USD$
and Drawn on a US Bank or branch.
✓ Payment by credit card preferred!

SPECIAL NOTES

✓ RETAILERS: Standard Discounts Available
✓ BACKORDERS: We Backorder all Out-of-
Stock Items Unless Otherwise Requested
✓ PRO FORMA INVOICES: Available on Request
✓ VIDEOS: NTSC Mode Only. Replacement only.
✓ For PAL mode videos contact our other offices:

European Office:
Adventures Unlimited, Pannewal 22,
Enkhuizen, 1602 KS, The Netherlands
http: www.adventuresunlimited.nl
Check Us Out Online at:
www.adventuresunlimitedpress.com

Please check: ☑

☐ This is my first order   ☐ I have ordered before   ☐ This is a new address

Name	
Address	
City	
State/Province	Postal Code
Country	
Phone day	Evening
Fax	Email

Item Code	Item Description	Price	Qty	Total

Please check: ☑

☐ Postal-Surface
☐ Postal-Air Mail
(Priority in USA)
☐ UPS
(Mainland USA only)

Subtotal ➠	
Less Discount-10% for 3 or more items ➠	
Balance ➠	
Illinois Residents 6.25% Sales Tax ➠	
Previous Credit ➠	
Shipping ➠	
Total (check/MO in USD$ only)➠	

☐ Visa/MasterCard/Discover/Amex

Card Number

Expiration Date

10% Discount When You Order 3 or More Items!

Comments & Suggestions	Share Our Catalog with a Friend